RAWN

CULTURE, THE HUMAN PLAN

Essays in the Anthropological Interpretation of Human Behavior

Charles C. Case

UNIVERSITY
PRESS OF
AMERICA

Copyright © 1977 by
University Press of America,Inc.℠
P.O. Box 19101, Washington, D.C. 20036

Printed in the United States of America

ISBN: 0-8191-0268-7 (Perfect)

Library of Congress Number: 82-45221

PREFACE

This book of essays presents some thoughts about human behavior that derive primarily from an anthropological perspective. It is not a research report and is not aimed at the scientific community, but rather at the undergraduate social science student or the interested layman. It is not a technical book and a considerable effort has been made to avoid jargon and specialized vocabularies, and to give a clear, simply expressed and personal presentation of the topic. Citations and references to particular theories and individuals have been deliberately avoided because they often confuse and distract from the flow of the discussion. Examples of exotic ethnographic materials have been limited in the belief that such examples many times mislead and obscure the basic theoretical thrust of anthropology. This should not imply there is no recognition of the complexities of the topic discussed or of the dangers of simplistic explanation. The challenge of this book is to present a simple straightforward jargon-free discussion of an immensely complex subject without oversimplifying it.

The focal message is an alternative theory of human behavior which challenges many of the concepts that are popular today. This theory derives from anthropology and the concept of culture and emphasizes the collective social and learned elements of human behavior rather than the innate aspects of some presumed "human nature." It runs counter to the popular concept of human behavior which stresses the individual autonomy of human activity and its dependence upon internal psychic processes. The psychic concept is so generally accepted however, that most Americans are so completely convinced that their behavior stems from their own unique beliefs, motivations, repressions, aggressions, and instincts that they no longer question this idea.

It is not that people have not heard of culture. On the contrary, the term has been extensively used during the last generation. The problem is that it has been misunderstood and relegated to a descriptive role in the treatment of human affairs. People are generally unaware that mankind, over thousands of years worked steadily toward the development of a comprehensive strategy for attacking the problems of human life, a strategy that, would guide and shape individual acts into successful and productive channels of behavior. The lives of millions upon millions of human beings have been formed by this cultural process, this human plan. But with the rise of large urban populations, mass migrations and modern nations, the visibility and understanding of the human plan became obscured and forgotten. Bringing this cultural factor to light again and explaining its structure and function constitute the content of this book.

CONTENTS

CHAPTER ONE

THE PROBLEM OF OUR AGE

Every age has its trials, its questions and its answers. Often the crucial issues are not obvious, not easily perceived, and merely identifying them becomes a major task in itself. But this is not the case today for the primary question of our time is very clear; how can we better understand and manage human affairs?

This is not a new problem. From the earliest days of human history, mankind has had to contend with the difficulties of controlling the actions of people, with maintaining group harmony, with managing quarrelsome and destructive individuals, and with conflicting interests. Individual behavior often seemed capricious, mysterious and baffling, and endless theories have been proposed to explain why people behaved the way they did. Some thought that supernatural beings, devils, evil spirits or gods manipulated and directed each human act. Others have explained behavior with instincts, hormones, vitamins, drugs, even ideal forms residing godlike in some great universal library of behavioral models. Religions, morals, values and belief systems were all created in an effort to direct and manage group and individual behavior. But the problem is far from resolved and on the contrary becomes more and more critical with each passing day. With all our discoveries and achievements, why are we still

1

plagued with wars, murders, crime, unhappiness, alcoholism, drug addiction, and mental and emotional malfunctioning?

This question is no longer one of idle speculation. Man has been caught in a desperate race to improve the management of his existence before he destroys himself. His is an existence increasingly punctuated by one crisis after another. Day by day, life unrolls like a great tapestry, revealing yet another set of surprises, another precipice, another waterfall. Man moves in a timeless theatre, watching his own history in shadowy outline on the screen before him, not knowing the plot or who the director is. He is baffled by how he got into his present condition and by his ability to do so little about it. Only occasionally does he realize that he has been sleepwalking along the narrow edge of a board fence, teetering and tottering along, suddenly filled with the certain dread that unexpectedly the whole thing will come crashing down.

The meaning of much of our experience is unclear. It is a mosaic of days without number and without pattern. People do not know how to translate it into expectations for the future. This is a considerable change from the past century with its slower pace and smaller volume of human activity. People then held in the main optimistic views about life. They had their poverty, pogroms, massacres, child labor, oppressed minorities, slums, disease, depressions and wars, but these were seen as temporary and regional. They saw the new industrial technology and scientific progress leading mankind along a relatively accessible path into a new era of peace and prosperity. Hard work and perseverance would ensure a better world for the future. The enemy was not man but nature. It was an age in which even the revolutionaries and anarchists envisioned utopias as possible and close at hand. Suffragette grandmothers were confident that votes for women would purify the political arena. The telegraph, the telephone, the electric light bulb, the x-ray and a hundred other products of discovery and invention kindled the highest hopes for the betterment of human life. Today we have our parliament of men, the proletariat as neighbors, radio and television in our homes, automobiles in our garages, and still all is not well. Nuclear energy has proved fraught with peril, the miracles of DDT have boomeranged and the computer threatens to become its own master.

A change has occurred and naive optimism has vanished to be replaced by caution and uncertainty. The newspapers more and more emphasize disaster, wars, and depressions, and print only vague and uncertain glimpses of anything giving cause for hope of improvement. They have not invented these crises but as global involvement has grown and communication facilities extended, there has been an increasing awareness and response to world conditions by the public. In a sense ignorance was a blessing because as it has become more difficult to hide the realities of the world condition, everyone has become more crisis oriented, and under the impact of repeated crises, more fearful and cynical.

The atmosphere of our time is ominous. This is the century when the poet, looking into the future, saw the possibility of the world ending not with a bang but a whimper. Little did he think that the bang was also possible. The oracles of the future forecast hard times ahead for us and harder times yet for our children and grandchildren if indeed there are any. There are fearful predictions of a massive global famine in an ever more densely populated world or a silent spring with no ear to notice as the life chains are poisoned by pesticidal residuals.

Pessimism is widespread for despite all man's knowledge, his experience and experiments, he is becoming mired deeper and deeper in a vast debacle of undetermined extent. He has grown more puzzled by his inability to understand what is happening to him, or to see any control and containment of the crushing uncertainty of human existence. Life seems to control him rather than he life and there is a growing conviction that man is incapable of successfully managing his own affairs.

The crisis in America is expressed in many ways, through individual protest, terrorist bombings, and the constant struggle for power between the citizens and the entrenched managers of government. It is even more directly expressed by the high incidence of alcoholism, drug addiction, criminal activity, and marriage failure. As if these problems were not enough, the damage to the personal emotional and mental well being of countless millions of people is revealed by the unhappiness, sense of failure, unsatisfactory personal relationships, loneliness, and lack of meaning in life that is rampant in our society. These afflictions are so common and so well documented that they have become just another boring recitation. They are so common that millions of people accept them not only as a reality of human life, but as human life.

But crisis is only part of the issue, the symptom. The real issue is how to reach a better understanding of the way humans generate their behavior. The fact that we are in crisis only emphasizes the urgency of this problem.

It is not that effort has not been expended to increase our knowledge about human behavior and to disseminate this knowledge. On the contrary, books and theories about the origin, structure, and modification of human behavior abound. College and professional lectures proliferate on every hand, each claiming to have found the final answers. We are drowned by innumerable books on how to save one's marriage, raise one's children, lose excess weight, become more intelligent, or attractive, or rich. How-to books cram every book store window and their production has become a massive and lucrative business in itself. But rather than resolving our problems all of this sudden concern with human behavior overwhelms and confuses us with its very volume and diversity.

Social protest has created two factions in America, those who still believe the mechanisms of democratic action can rescue the situation, and those who believe that it is too late and only a complete restructuring of society through revolutionary activity will bring about the necessary changes. Although both parties obstensibly seek the same goal, a better society for everyone, they have become bitter enemies fighting each other rather than the common problem.

Beneath the surface however, is a critical issue which is closely related to the total viability of the present social system. The survival of any society is dependent upon the success with which its members are able to strike a balance between externally maintained social order and internal self-regulation. While people in general move towards greater and greater self-regulation as they mature, societies move toward more and more dependence upon external maintained social order. To avoid self-destruction, every society must provide both the means for members to move from externally ordered behavior to self-regulation, and the experience necessary for this process to become a reality. The struggle in America is over this issue.

As a result of the crisis in America over external regulation and self-regulation, and the failure of both, a new phenomena, the counseling profession, has come into being. Millions of people recognize that something is amiss with themselves and seek help with the management of their lives. This need for expert personal help represents the magnitude of the crisis in America.

For many generations people with personal problems went to their church or minister for help, and concern about the nature of human behavior originated within philosophy and religion. Today most people no longer blame fate or supernaturals for their predicaments, but look to the intra-psychic functioning of human nature, the basic psychology of man, for their answers. Psychology and psychiatry have replaced the church and philosophy, and many psychologists now consider human behavior their exclusive domain. That this view has gained credence is demonstrated by the fact that the legal courts of the land rely more and more heavily upon the testimony of experts in the psychological sciences.

Human nature has now replaced the supernatural spirits of former times as the instigator of behavior. It is commonly accepted that mankind is naturally aggressive, vicious, cruel, and warlike, and that behavior is determined by the psychic mechanisms of frustration, ambition, love, hate, envy, kindness, beliefs, depression, and anger. Each human being is viewed as irrational and self-centered where these qualities exist in constant agitation, struggling for expression, and battling for control of each scrap of behavior. The outward expression of behavior becomes a compromise between the individual's warring instinctual feeling states, and the demands of society that he repress these desires. How a child experiences and manages these feeling states may warp and twist him in such a fashion that he can suffer permanent damage and be unable to function successfully as an adult. The individual is thought to be basically evil, an animal whose passions must be strictly controlled since they are always on the verge of breaking out and creating havoc in the individual's life. These passions are so powerful and the struggle to control them so traumatic that if they momentarily escape, the person will be overcome with guilt feelings, and immense psychological damage will result.

It sometimes comes as a great surprise to learn that there are other theories and data about behavior besides those presented by the psychological sciences. These theories do not always agree with the psychological explanations of human behavior, and in fact often are contradictory or incompatible with them. Anthropologists, for example, deny that human nature is that responsible for our behavior. While the peculiar and distinguishing characteristics of the human being as a physiological and psychologically functioning organism are important to understand, they are not the determinant factors in the making of war, or becoming mentally and emotional incapacitated, nor do they dictate any human conduct in the sense often implied. Man does not come into being with his behavior determined by preformed acts hidden somewhere in the recesses of the brain. He is not equipped with any intrinsic mechanism already programmed into aggressions, motivations, affections, and frustrations. Mankind is not innately good or evil, aggressive or kind, loving or hateful, jealous or promiscuous. On the contrary mankind has invented and developed the way it behaves.

Man is what he becomes and what he becomes is determined by the experiences that he has in life.

One of the reasons then that we face a world of crisis, and seem so unable to cope with it, stems from some of the misleading concepts that people have about the basis of their own behavior. As long as they continue to believe that the mainsprings of behavior are individual and psychological, they will continue to be baffled by what is happening to them. Mankind long ago discovered the shortcomings of their own biological and psychological equipment and began to replace human nature with another system of managing behavior, the cultural system.

There is a very significant difference between the cultural approach to human behavior and the psychological approach. In the anthropological view the determining factors in behavior are seen as created by man, but external to the individual. In the psychological view they are thought to lie in the functioning of the individual's intrapsychic mechanisms. In the psychological view it is believed that a person behaves the way he does because he is neurotic, psychotic, intelligent, unintelligent, frustrated, aggressive, or repressed. In the cultural explanation a person behaves the way he does largely because that is the way he has been taught is appropriate in his society.

It is the purpose of this book to explore the cultural explanation of human behavior and to make the cultural concept meaningful and relevant to both individual activity and to the world crisis. It would be naive to think that merely by re-examining the concept of culture and its relationship to behavior that all the ills of the world can be alleviated. But on the other hand it is doubtful that world conditions will be significantly improved without a better grasp of the nature and function of culture.

CHAPTER TWO

THE MANY MEANINGS OF CULTURE

The cultural view of human behavior derives largely from the work of individuals who have lived and studied in a multitude of behavioral systems. This view contrasts sharply with the more widely accepted psychological concept with its focus on the intrapsychic processes of the individual. Although the idea of culture has been widely recognized as the major contribution that anthropology has made to a theory of human behavior since Edward Tyler presented his now famous definition in 1871, it does not mean there have been no arguments about its meaning and significance. These disagreements are of two kinds: unawareness of cultural theory, and unwillingness to accept culture on an equal basis with intrapsychic processes in understanding human actions. In addition, the petty quarrels over a precise meaning of culture, both within anthropology and without, have diluted and obscured the impact of the concept. To add still further confusion the word passed into the everyday vocabulary where it took on still other meanings.

These other meanings present some of the major obstacles in grasping the full significance of culture in human affairs. Everyone is convinced that he knows what culture is. It has become a commonplace metaphor to which anyone can attach his inadequate thoughts or clever opinions. It litters the conversation of the sophisticate, the jet setter, the opera buff, and those who are enthralled with the arts, manners, and witty chatter. To be cultured has come to mean to be knowledgeable about painting, music, opera, dance, and literature. It has often become the symbol of snobbery which has justified colonialism, conquest, and imperialism.

For the world traveler, culture conveys folkways and traditions, the pretty costumes, folksongs, strange rituals of faraway people, the superficial, exotic, and bizarre. Dabs of cultural knowledge add spice to the cocktail party, a kind of conversational confetti one can casually strew about as one speaks knowingly of rubbing noses in an igloo, or eating fried grasshoppers with the Shoshone.

For intellectuals, culture has become the scapegoat for all the ills of modern life, the alienation of youth, the crime rate, and the growing divorce problem, although just how culture is at fault no one seems to know. Culture, like a species of modern day sorcery, has replaced primitive magic as a kind of secret spell that makes people ill, or evil, or marriages fail.

Scientists use the cultural concept in still another way. They describe the different societies and activities found around the world, relate what other people are like, and reveal what they eat, and what they think. It is used to compare similarities and differences among societies, to explain the clash of nations, the effects of exploration or commerce, and the shock of strange customs. Massive attempts have been made to record all the various traits, characteristics, and behavioral activities engaged in by the human species. Every conceivable form of tool, every institution, custom, habit, and language of mankind has been described, analyzed, and compared. Culture has been called modal behavior, the super ego, the collective unconscious, norms, design for living, even sublimations. For a long while it was even portrayed as superorganic, omnipotent, and eternal, floating royally over the inert world of the inorganic and the simpler world of the organic. Here it operated with its own laws, directing · the course of mankind independent of the physical and psychological worlds. Finally some bold individual took the obvious step and declared culture to be nothing at all, a mental construct found only in the mind of the beholder with no reality in itself. This concept has been mangled and mutilated, torn apart and put together, praised and damned. It has been slighted, ignored, and even occasionally discarded upon the junkpile of broken down momentoes of human thought.

It is obvious that many people either never grasped the full implications of Tyler's original definition or refused to accept it. Tyler stated quite explicitly that culture was "that complex whole which includes knowledge, belief, art, law, morals, custom, and any other capabilities and habits acquired by man as a member of society." In that statement he clearly indicated the integrative, holistic nature of culture, the same concept that was so enthusiastically received many years later when restated by the Gestalist and Korzbski.

There is no question then, that there is confusion about, as well as a failure to grasp the implications of the culture concept. Despite all the different meanings that have been given to culture, there is nevertheless a common thread of an idea that emerges. Different words may be used, folkways, mores, history, or civilization, but all imply that culture is a description of traditions transmitted from person to person, from generation to generation through time. One can hardly quarrel with this. It is the next stop that creates difficulties for it is easy to imply that traditions and customs also cause behavior. People smoke, make war, or fashion pottery because it is the custom. Giving causal powers to a description of customs raises a host of objections and steps on many toes. Such a concept comes into direct conflict with many other theories about the origins of human activity. For example, if one believes that supernatural beings are responsible for an individual's behavior, or that some autonomous self exists like a tiny internal dictator, or that the ghost of the dead, or witches or instincts, or physiochemical processes, or stimulus and response mechanisms are responsible for behavior, then culture as a causal agent is challenging, disconcerting, and threatening.

Indeed people often react to these claims of causal powers by insisting that the cultural concept is vague, oversimplified, and even a pernicious form of stereotyping. They protest and resist the generalizing of those who use the terms. They want to concentrate upon the individual and the particular, failing to find the concept useful in understanding how specific individuals and societies function. They want to know why one man beats his wife, becomes an alcoholic, and commits suicide, while another man writes novels, composes music, and races automobiles. They do not believe culture offers an adequate explanation of this level of behavior.

There is also criticism that culture is an abstraction that has been unconsciously idealized. It is insisted that concepts generalized from a wide array of specific behavior cannot in themselves act. Only individuals behave. These critics declare that culture is not an object of empirical reality like a rock or a tree but is an epiphenomena. Since it does not have an empirical nature, it cannot be a causal agent as often implied, and can only describe human behavior, not explain it. Furthermore, if it is super-organic, subjective, ethereal, and detached, how does it manifest itself in concrete customs and behavior? How does it become translated into specific human activity?

There are obvious limitations to the usefulness of any description of customs or mores. Attempts to use abstractions like traditions or customs as explanations of actual behavior have been unconvincing and weak in clarifying the dynamic processes underlying overt behavior. In a world full of domestic turmoil and international crises, descriptions are no longer enough.

They are equivalent to the descriptions of illness that formed the bulk of medical knowledge a century ago. For ages, mankind was plagued by innumerable ills and disease which seemingly appeared out of nowhere to strike down the strong, the weak, the child, or the adult. To the father or mother who watched their loved ones fever and die, illness seemed mysterious, capricious, god-determined, beyond understanding, the machinations of forces beyond human grasp or control. Descriptions of smallpox, no matter how full or accurate, did not console the living. Vast schemes were concocted rent with superstition and magic to combat the effects of illness.

But once the bacterial nature of disease was discovered a whole new understanding of illness became available. The transmission of bacteria from person to person, the importance of hygiene, the need for isolation in treatment and prevention of disease were suddenly clear.

Just as it once was difficult to explain, without the germ theory, how large numbers of people might simultaneously suffer from smallpox or diphtheria, so it is equally difficult to explain many aspects of human behavior without an adequate theory of culture. Something does exist that makes people in a society act in many similar ways, that creates recognizable collective behavior. Making the concept of culture meaningful as an explanation of behavior rather than as a description of behavior is not a simple matter but it is not a hopeless one.

Culture as a factor in human behavior needs reexamination. The old definitions and concepts are too vauge, misleading, and hopelessly confused. While not necessarily inaccurate, they are difficult to operationalize and put into a meaningful explanatory theory. But because of the commonplaceness of culture, a theory of culture runs the risk of being simplistic and obvious.

CHAPTER THREE

THE GENERAL NATURE OF CULTURE

The General Nature of Culture

The purpose of this chapter is to present a closer examination of the concept of culture and to develop a theoretical statement about the fundamental nature of culture. The use of culture as a descriptive device for portraying the many different societies of the world provides only limited understanding of human activity. It is too broad, too general, and too non-specific to explain the intricacies and complexities of much of human behavior. In fact, it does not explain how behavior comes into being at all, but merely relates what has happened after it has occurred and draws some relationships between different aspects of behavior. Here we shall attempt to make a finer grained analysis of culture, isolate some basic elements, and relate these elements directly and specifically to human acts. We will show how these basic elements are tied in to increasingly more complex linkages until a network of cultural units is created which encompass most of human activity.

Culture is only one of several factors involved in the shaping of human existence. Setting, situation, people, and communication also are important. The

15

setting where human activity occurs includes the physical conditions of place, size, shape, and the totality
of the environmental features operating upon the human
arena. This may be a house, a ship, an athletic field,
a tribal territory, or a field of battle. The activity that
takes place in that setting is both a response to and a
creator of the situation, that historical moment with its
problems, floods, wars, tennis games, and political
campaigns, that are part of human life. All situations
involve some problem that is in the process of resolution. People are the actors resolving out the conflict
upon the stage provided by the setting. Individuals,
groups, and groups of groups, and all the things associated with the biology of people, their number, their
organizational structure, their sex and age distribution,
and their roles and statuses, are factors in the creation
and resolution of human problems. People interact
through language in order to facilitate the solution of
the problems that perplex them. Otherwise there would
be a silent pantomine played by deaf and blind actors.

The plans and techniques that are used by the people
of a group to deal with the problems that occur within
the setting, and which they share with each other
through communication, becomes the culture of the
group. The relation of culture to setting we call knowledge, to situation we call strategy, to people, social
structure, and to communication, language. Culture
is the element that ties all these factors together into
that which is human life.

Culture penetrates and shapes every human life.
It engulfs each person totally, overwhelmingly. Yet
people are seldom aware of its existence. They do not
understand its effect upon their lives and their behavior. They believe they act out of their own private
independent volition, out of the whims and fantasies of
their own individuality. Culture has been misunderstood, its nature misconstrued. Confused with customs
or traditions, folkways or mores, its significance has
been concealed and its role in human life overshadowed
by the emphasis on psychological processes.

In a very fundamental sense culture is the most
human part of man's existence. It encompasses those

aspects of being that are learned, those regularities that are acquired, those things that are gained through association with other humans. It is the social heritage that has developed out of the biological responses in the life process. It is the web of relationships holding people together in viable groups. It is the structure of predictability in the behavior of the members of society which tells each person who he is and who other people are. It provides the techniques for dealing with life problems, and for directing the shape of one's existence.

Man is not equipped with some intrinsic psychic mechanism that tells him how to conduct his life nor is he directed by some supernatural being, god or devil, or by the conjunctions of the stars or the phases of the moon. These do not compel his behavior. Man has developed his own capability to shape behavior based on the experience of his own existence. He is responsible for his own acts. As each man matures and participates in life, he transforms his life into human meaning through the enculturation and enactment of the culture in which he exists.

There is far more to culture than the mere passing on of some customs, some tools and institutions. It consists of more than recitation of what has already occurred, of how strange Amazonian Indians make blow guns or shrink heads, of tattooing, tabus, basketry designs, or of kinship designations. These describe acts and artifacts which are the result of culture projected into behavior, but they are not culture. Behind the customs and the tools, the social habits and behavior, lies the framework of a plan, the human plan, the plan of culture.

This plan is not passive but is a guiding system, a behavioral map, a grammar of behavior. It leads one to places unsuspected, by paths unknown and perhaps even against one's will. It is constantly present working to shape behavior into its outward form.

Natural codes exist throughout the universe and are expressed in the biological, chemical and physiological orders. But man has constructed a fourth, the most complex of all. Like other codes it provides each individual and each society with both general and detailed instructions and directions for enacting concrete behavior. It is an active process that channels and shapes happenings into specific human acts. Customs and folkways are only the description of human activity, but they are not what culture is. They provide no more understanding of culture than the external facade of a skyscraper indicates how the building manages to stand upright, of how it came to be, of the framework that lies hidden between the walls and floors. Culture is the construct behind overt behavior. Like a blueprint or work schedule it is prior, basic, and necessary to any action. Like the plays and rules of football or the recipe of a cake, it determines the final result. But the product is also a part of the cultural plan. Culture is the means, artifacts and behavior the ends.

Most explanations of how a person carries out a behavioral act use a three stage lineal model. For example, playing the piano includes the initial desire to play, the physical act of fingering the keys, and a product called music. This model very briefly then consists of stimulus, behavior, and description.

The concept of culture is almost invariably used in connection with the third or descriptive phase of this model if it is used at all. Nevertheless, culture is also supposed to influence in some way how people act. When people bow on greeting, or shake hands, or hug each other, these behaviors are said to be determined by custom. But it is never stated how the custom of shaking hands results in hand shaking.

The theory of culture offered here, however, presents a somewhat different method for explaining the relationship of culture to a behavioral act. The crucial difference is that culture is placed not at the descriptive end of the behavioral episode but rather at the beginning. The cultural theory of behavior would rearrange the sequence of behavior elements as stimulus, a cultural model, behavior, and a description of this behavior as a custom. The analogy with piano playing restructures the lineal sequence then as desire to play, reading of a musical score, the fingering of the keys, and the musical product. This then enables us to see the part culture has in shaping behavior, and removes it from the passive descriptive role to which it is usually assigned. Furthermore it is evident that without the cognitive or physical existence of the musical score, the individual cannot in fact produce music. Nor can he produce any other act without an analogous behavioral score. This score, or as it is called here, the cultural model, is the guide to behavior. It is the ability to construct, use and transmit such cultural guides that constitutes the single most significant human capability.

The structure of language provides a further illustration. As every person matures he acquires an immense list of words which he learns to put together into meaningful utterances. He does this through the device of grammar, the instructions that lie behind speech. He does not necessarily learn either words or grammar consciously or purposefully. He simply absorbs them as he grows and increases the scope of his vocal and auditory capacities. It is unlikely he will invent many of the words or much of the grammar he uses, for he depends upon what has already been developed by other people. What he can say, how he says it and what it means are all related to the nature of the particular speech elements which he inherits. Even what he can think and what he can perceive are influenced and shaped by his particular language. Regardless of how creative one thinks he is, language is always learned from others and the existing vocabulary and grammar shape the nature of the vocal utterances by acting as a set of instructions or plans guiding actual expression. Literally, one cannot speak without the guiding plan of grammar.

. The grammar of a language is a pre-solution to the problem of how to arrange sounds so they can convey meaning. A pre-solution is based on the assumption that problems recur and its task is to ensure that a trial-and-error process does not have to be repeated each time the same problem arises. Each society has already organized, categorized, summarized, and abstracted the experience of countless lives into useful data and instructions which have been turned into problem-solving plans. By anticipating the recurring problems and situations in life, it makes instructional plans for handling them available to the individual member of the group in a profusion far beyond his individual capacity to create. These plans become historic habits carried on from generation to generation, as internalized as the grammar which controls man's speech.

These cultural plans are seldom simple. The process by which they have become what they are at any given moment is not simple. They represent the accumulated residual of the complex behavior of hundreds of generations of people. Growing food in the desert of the American Southwest, for example, is difficult, perilous and close to impossible. But in spite of the extremes of cold and heat, of limited surface water, and little rain, the Hopi and the Zuni have managed to live and thrive in the area. Through long experience they have developed behavior models which tell them where and when to plant seeds and how to produce a successful crop: on the north side of the hill shielded from the sun; on the south side if the weather is cloudy; in the gullies if there is a drought; on the slopes if there is flooding. Each possibility is considered and provided for; each contingency is met with its own rule. These models offer the most effective solution to the problems which crowd upon them, are the best they have been able to devise with the limited technology available. They are not to be taken lightly, to be altered and tossed aside at someone's whim; they are considered vital and are greatly valued. To ensure that they are understood and followed, many of them are ritualized into complex ceremonies, which, to the uninformed are often thought to be merely religious. Indeed, they often are deeply charged with emotional attributes. Without these sacred plans, some people would fail to cope with the difficulties of uncertain rainfall or the complex relationship of planting to the changing seasons. They would not store corn for the winter or prepare the fields in the spring. They would become hungry and ill, and others would have to share and care for them lest they starve. The existence of all would be threatened. Threatening behavior cannot be tolerated. Neither can people who do not understand and obey the rules be tolerated.

Culture is complex, and its analysis is also complex. The cultural plans that people use are composed of many different facets and it is not always easy to understand them and to see exactly how they fit together. To use an analogy, life is a game in which there are players, plays, status, roles, structure, and instructions. The method of organizing this "life game" is through sharing a body of instructions. Every society evolves and borrows such a set of directives to enable its members to exist and to cooperate--in essence, to play the game of life. Members cannot behave efficiently or interact successfully without following these mutually understood guides. What they know, what they do, what they discuss, and how they interact are all dependent upon the instructions which each individual knows and shares with others.

The result of these instructions are analogous to the effect produced by the rules of any game. To believe they have no causal effect upon the conduct of the players or the course of the game is equivalent to believing that the rules of football have no effect upon the specific activity of that game. Whatever the means by which games are affected by rules is the way life is affected by culture. Obviously the rules and instructions of games both describe them and at the same time shape them. The fact that culture consists basically of mental plans and ideas existing in the minds of separate individuals does not make culture a form of psychological reductionism any more than the rules of a game make them reductionist. Like the rules of any game, cultural plans exist and their purpose is to enable the game of life at the human level to be played.

It has been suggested that culture is a script one follows to create behavior, and one behavioral therapy uses this analogy in its treatment processes. But a script implies some characteristics that are significally different from culture. The most important of these is the implication that culture is the mechanical recitation of a previously written page. This is erroneous. The difference between a script and the cultural model might be illustrated as the difference between a football game and the staging of a theatrical play. In football the script of the game is not totally predetermined, only the rules and instructions which the players use are predetermined. What actually occurs on the field at any given moment is a result of a host of factors the most important of which is the selection of previous play activity and its execution.

In a theatrical play on the other hand, one reads what the script presents and the outcome is already known. The analogy with a script then might be more correct if the actors were given certain general instructions about what the purpose of the drama was and then put out on the stage to improvise as various situations developed within the general meaning of the script. While it is true that culture has a tendency to reduce much of life to the regularity of a script, the constantly changing cast of characters and shifting environmental conditions make it impossible for human existence ever to be that set. The success of culture as an adaptive device is precisely that point; that is, to provide a general guide that is flexible enough to permit appropriate behavior in a large number of specific instances.

The common concept of culture as nothing more than customs must be discarded. To see man acting, to observe his behavior, and subsequently to call such acts culture is only the beginning step toward understanding the nature of culture. If culture is to be accepted as a dynamic functioning factor in behavior then it must be seen as immediate, participating, and invariably present as a prerequisite to behavior. Culture is not the description abstracted from the observation of human activity; it is not norms, or statistical averages, but the cognitive plans that are present before activity occurs. Culture is not the result of behavior, but a determinate of behavior.

The Specific Nature of Culture

The common conception of culture is too general to be useful in an operational sense. Consequently culture has never been accepted very seriously in any theory of human behavior although lip service has been paid to its importance. It has been treated as an interesting but hardly explanatory concept.

To make the idea of culture more meaningful, we can think of it as composed of smaller more comprehensible particles. These particles act as separate, distinguishable and unitized entities which can be put together with other such entities to create larger, more complex behavioral segments. I have called the smallest meaningful unit of culture a nomeme, a nomeme being a single instructional phrase that guides an individual through a single behavioral act. It is a precise directive that exists in the individual's mind in readiness as a plan of action. Nomemes are the enduring self-instructions that enable a person to behave and which give the individual's activity consistency, and group behavior, its commonality.

The essence of the nomeme is its propositional and enabling capacity; that is, the use of a nomeme results in some kind of cognitive, affective, or behavioral action and the consequent resolution of some problem. Nomemes are structured in such a way that if one follows the instructions they contain some act transpires. This may be as simple as "sit down", "speak softly", "eat", or "run", but enacting each of these nomemes enables the person to accomplish some segment of behavior.

The ability to construct, use and transmit nomemes depends upon the capacity of the brain to condense a mass of behavioral experience into a single incisive phrase that will be useable in some future behavioral episode. Nomemes represent the causal link between mental and behavioral activity and they are dependent upon the functional ability of the mind to recognize, categorize, generalize, and grasp cause and effect relationships. This involves a highly developed sense for discrimination, for sorting, for grouping, and naming. The human mind constantly searches and analyzes the stream of sensory experience that reaches it for material that can be transformed into useable nomemes.

The construction of nomemes is only one of the cognitive steps leading to behavior. These steps include the development of simple sensory or image models, the construction of specific nomemic phrases from the data available, and the selection and enactment of the appropriate nomeme.

Sensory models are isomorphic with the kind of reality recorded by the various sense organs and include such a variety of things as the image of a tree, the auditory image of a word, a smell, or a feeling. These images are generalized but contain the basic identifying characteristics of the reality they relate to. They provide stored empirical data and are essential in the preliminary identification processes of the brain.

The second step consists of analyzing and using the data contained in the sensory images. This includes identifying, comparing, and organizing the data and evaluating its potency. It includes grasping causal relationships, creating categorical groups, and naming.

The development of the actual behavioral model or nomeme is one of the more critical functions of the human brain. This requires a recognition of the problem, a knowledge of what needs to be done, the development of a step by step series of actions, an awareness of what each step will accomplish, and a model of the desired outcome. Nomemes must be structured in such a way that they can be operationalized, are not contradictory and are progressively ordered so that activities which are dependent upon the completion of prior acts occur in the proper sequence. Nomemes are derived from the data provided by the experience of each individual but more importantly, by the accumulated experience of the social group to which the person belongs. They are stored in readiness as traditions, rituals, or habits. They are ideal plans of action but their fit to the conditions of any particular unfolding situation is only approximate.

Nomemes have a distinctive propositional and semantic structure which gives them their particular instructional meaning. They are not merely statements of fact or descriptions of events. They do not simply pass on knowledge and information or relate one's emotional condition or the time of day. Their function is to create behavior and each nomemic phrase, whether long or short, is arranged in a particular order distinguishing the actor, the action, and the acted upon. While this may not always be the same order as found in an English sentence the result is the same. The actor in fact may only be implied, but the action is clear.

The objective, which is expressed as a nomeme, may be as simple as desiring to open a door. But this simple directive may require numerous instrumental nomemes before the door is actually opened. The person must move to a position in front of the door, the key must be removed from the pocket, inserted into the keyhole, turned in the correct direction, the door knob turned, the door pushed open, the key removed and returned to the pocket. Thus the larger behavioral episode is made up of many smaller acts each of which requires a separate nomemic instruction. Each nomeme must distinguish clearly between the sub acts within the total episode and each nomeme must proceed and follow a correct order in the sequence.

To a person who is familiar with doors and keys this may seem like an unnecessarily complex explanation of a very simple act. Yet these are the steps necessary to unlock a door and to a person unfamiliar with keys and doors they can present a baffling problem until he learns the appropriate nomemes.

Nomemes are created to manage actual situations in an individual's life and are a response to the factual aspects of the real world and their effect upon the person. But before action nomemes can be developed they must be preceded by the recognition and evaluation of certain basic situations and conditions in the surrounding world. These states and conditions pertain to fundamental logical properties of time, space, and quality and are evaluated by a process of contrastive scaling. They involve self-awareness in terms of body position and size relative to other objects and organisms which one encounters in the environment. These fundamental distinctions include distinguishing between before and after, front from behind, right from left and above from below. They also include the ability to differentiate larger from smaller, longer from shorter, weaker from stronger and other opposable conditions. Making these distinctions is directly related to the necessity of distinguishing between dangerous and harmless, between animals that are larger or stronger than one, from those that are weaker, or body positions that are more vulnerable than others. Recognizing that a lion is more threatening than a cat requires tools for judging size, distance and strength. "Behind one" produces reactions that are different from "in front of one" because of the susceptibility of each person to surprise attack from the rear or above. Conceptual awareness of the meaning of each of these situations is not confined to a particular instance but are generalizable. Concern about the danger of night in contrast to the light of day carries over into expressions of fear regarding dark forest, jungles, and unlighted streets and buildings. Emotional significance is attached to the nomemes that are created to manage these situations because there is a recognition of the meaning each has for the well being of the individual.

All cultural systems include within their structure the classification of some of these universal opposable categories, although the emotional treatment of them may vary widely. Non-opposable attributes of the real world such as color systems, plant or animal types, or landscape features are also classified. Many of these are particular, unique, and nontransferrable such as distinguishing types of snow in the arctic, or kinds of horses or camels in Arabia, or mental malfunctioning in a hospital. While almost everyone can respond to large or small, front or back, not everyone is familiar with the various kinds of snow that an Eskimo encounters.

All nomemes exist to facilitate behavior necessitated by some situation affecting the individual. Once the nature of the situation has been determined upon the basis of the kind of situational data that the brain has received, the selection of a specific nomeme for enactment is dependent upon how well the existing nomemes fit the problem. The nomeme a baboon uses when a lion appears close by will result in a simple non-specific warning signal expressing an emotional state. The information imparted is elementary because the primary function of this type of signal is to alert other members of the group. It then becomes their responsibility to determine the nature and extent of the danger and respond accordingly. In that sense the baboon's scream is no different from the toot of an automobile horn. The horn tells nothing about the size or speed of the vehicle but merely alerts other drivers to some impending danger.

Object specific nomemes are much more informative and express a more precise identification of objects and events in the environment. While the direct information conveyed may not be great, the indirect information is considerably more than merely expressing a warning. When a human sees a dangerous ground predator, he may emit either a simple alarm scream or an object specific signal. A simple signal will not tell whether the predator is a lion or a leopard, a very critical distinction since one climbs trees and the other does not. An object specific signal may still only be a scream but it will be different for each animal, and consequently it has far greater survival effect although still highly generalized.

Symbolic nomemes on the other hand provide a far more precise classification of the objects and events in the external world and vastly increase the amount of information conveyed. Naming is the critical factor. All complex animals have sensory awareness, and recognition and categorization capabilities, but only humans can name. Naming is a distinctive symbolic activity involving the attachment of a consistent but arbitrary linguistic sign to some object, action, or emotional state. To name means that the individual possesses a nomeme for consistently labeling particular objects and events. This nomeme secures its effectiveness from the collective agreement among the members of an interacting group.

Without names, objects and actions exist only as sensory images in the mind. Names can be substituted for the sensory image in the cognitive processes and consequently named objects can be more easily managed than unnamed objects. But the real value of naming is demonstrated when concepts are being transferred from person to person. Sensory images must be drawn or represented in some objective fashion to be communicated, but once a name has been agreed upon, it can be transmitted and manipulated rapidly and efficiently between two or more persons. Shouting the specific word 'lion' is obviously more effective than simply emitting a scream and running for a tree.

Although each nomeme is a separate instructional statement the fact that it is rarely possible for a single act to resolve any human problem means that nomemes seldom occur in isolation. Rather they are joined to other nomemes in a series or chain. A set of interlinked and ordered nomemes forms a nomolary or recipe which leads an individual through a series of related acts to some solution. All individual nomemes fit into these nomolaries and patterns, and are constantly reviewed and tested for effectiveness and logical fit so that there is a congruence between conceptual construct and behavioral activity. New nomemes are measured against the patterns of existing nomemes for effectiveness in producing successful behavior. In most societies this process has distilled out over time a body of nomemes that have proved to be more effective than others, and which we call culture.

Nomemes can be categorized into two broad classes, those that might be thought of as personal and those that are collective or cultural. In a strict sense all nomemes are personal and idionomemic because each individual is a biologically and physically distinct and separate entity. Therefore nomemes exist only within the neurological structure provided by the organic parameters of each person. There is no membranic tissue that joins individual to individual and no sharing of internal psychological events except through the medium of communication. Each person develops his own private networks of nomemes and these only become cultural when other individuals also use the same or similar nomemes. Idionomemes are expressed as the mannerisms and characteristics that distinguish individuals from each other. These include personal gestures, vocabulary choices, clothing, and food preferences, and so on. They arise out of the unique historic incidents of each person's life and the particular biological characteristics of each person.

Culture on the other hand consists of all the nomemes and nomolaries that are shared by a group of people. Each nomeme is an allonomeme in the sense that each is a variation of some central concept held by the members of the society. To be considered cultural a nomeme not only must be held collectively but must persist over time and be transmitted from generation to generation.

Just as different kinds of nomemes exist, the actions they relate to are also of different types. Essentially there are three kinds of behavior possible: individual, interrelated and dependent, and interrelated and independent. The latter is represented by a foursome of golfers who employ a common set of tools, techniques and nomemes. But the physical acts used in golf are not directly dependent upon the actions of others and there is little interdependence among the players in so far as the game itself is concerned. The outcome of what one player does is not related directly to what another player is doing. The game of golf uses common but not interdependent rules.

Football or basketball are completely different. In these games each physical act is directly and immediately influenced by what several other players are doing at the same time. How one runs, blocks or catches a pass are all dependent upon the actions of other players. The behavior and the nomemes are thus interrelated and interdependent.

Individual behavior is simply that which involves only a single person and is neither shared nor interdependent. The nomemes that form a cultural system are so numerous that no individual ever knows or uses all those available anymore than a speaker knows all the words in his language. Culture does not mean that everyone is reading exactly the same script and that every individual is interchangeable with every other. What it does mean is that there is a body of instructions available to the members of a society which enables them to interact and coordinate their behavior even though each of them is an individual with his own capabilities, desires, and problems. Thus culture is neither the particular marriage ceremony or the exotic native dance but the nomemes which the participants share which guide them through the behavioral episodes in the ceremony or dance.

It is difficult for a person to generate action without having in mind the anticipated result of a particular behavior. The nomemic series must include not only the guides for each sequential step but a model of the expected outcome as well. If this were not so, there would be no way for the person to know if he had acted correctly or if in fact he had completed an act at all.

On the other hand it is easy to see the end result of action without always understanding the process. Anyone can admire a well turned pot or a beautifully fashioned spear point, but it is quite a different matter to produce one. To translate the visual model one has in mind into an actual artifact often requires understanding many auxiliary factors. In making the spear point it is necessary for example to recognize the differences between various kinds of lithic materials, and to know which stone is brittle and which is tough. One must know where to find the proper stone, how to chip and grind it to the desired shape and when the point is finished, one must know how to fasten it firmly to a wooden shaft. Eventually one must know how to use the spear either to throw or to thrust. Still that is not all, since the kind of spear one makes, whether small or large, heavy or light, depends upon what animal one is seeking and what skills one has as a hunter. While the objective of spear making is an evening meal, there are many steps between the first visual model and the final result. A vast series of nomemes and nomolaries must be developed, learned and enacted before there will be meat on the table. This is the reason why complex activities are so often formalized in procedural manuals or elaborate rituals to ensure that no act will be forgotten or performed incorrectly.

It is obvious that the operational expression of any nomeme or nomolary does not result in a mechanical reproduction of behavior or that actual behavior is ever an exact duplication of the cultural nomeme. Instead it is merely an approximation of various degrees of exactness, for the less clear the nomeme in the person's mind the less exact the result. Man is not a robot and the fact that he employs cultural nomemes does not make him the slave of a cultural determinism anymore than the use of a spear makes him a servant to the spear. Various levels of skill, strength, agility, intelligence, endurance, and interest mediate between the nomemic pattern and its expression in behavior.

Furthermore since the total body of nomemes changes over a period of time, individual responses differ correspondingly. No two individuals hold exactly the same interpretation of the same nomeme. Even if it were possible to share the same understanding, people vary in their ability to reproduce precisely the particular behavior associated with a nomeme because of the differences produced by age, sex, and personal experience. Even the same person cannot enact a given nomeme exactly the same on two different occasions. Situations themselves are never twice the same, nor do any two people hold exactly the same total set of nomolaries. While there is a general sharing of the culture by all members of the social group, no individual behaves in accordance with every directive found in his society. What does exist is a vast body of idionomemes, many of which overlap with those held by other people. The result is a mass of individual behavior much of which coincides with the behavior of other persons. It is the fact that there is some commonality and overlap that enables us to say the culture exists.

This does not mean that contradictory situations will not occur, that two different sets of nomemes may not be competing simultaneously for the individual's attention. But since only one nomeme at a time can be enacted, a decision has to be made. While the woman is preparing corn meal to make bread, a child gets hurt or her husband wants to make love. What she decides to do is determined by previous experience with this situation and the nomemes she has already devised. She will know that her husband can wait but to leave the bread too long while she nurses the child will result in burnt bread and much wasted effort. Recurrent use of a nomeme makes its selection more habitual and consequently a nomeme that has become habitual may take precedence over one that is more effective.

Non-productive or counter-productive nomemes can be learned by individuals as readily as productive nomemes. This may occur when a person receives erroneous information or misinterprets what he receives. Man is also deceived by the immediacy and intensity of his experience into constructing erroneous nomemes. The results of many behavioral acts often do not become available for evaluation until long after the action has taken place and hence cannot be used to alter or discard a non-productive nomeme. A primary function of the social group is to evaluate and restrain the production of inappropriate nomemes.

Culture is neither rules or norms although often confused with both. Rules may be nomemes but nomemes are not necessarily rules. Rules imply the imposition of restraints upon a person's behavior and subsequent punishment for nonconformity. Because there are so many wrong ways of trying to solve a problem, rules often have a restrictive and negative connotation. But nomemes exist to accomplish some task and are no more restrictive than the recipe for a cake or the blueprints for a building. They may exist in negative form but their primary purpose is to provide positive instructions in such a way that negative instructions are not needed.

Neither is culture equivalent to "norms," since norms imply that culture is derived from the statistical occurrence of some behavioral trait. But the statistical occurrence of a trait is irrelevant since this only measures the number of times an event has taken place and does not explain how the act came into being at all. Since "norms" are derived from the observation of behavior, and nomemes precede behavior it is evident that they are two different things.

Principles and Values

Every nomeme is embedded in a string of related nomemes or a nomolary. The specific nomeme directs a single act, the nomolary a series of acts whose purpose is to resolve a larger problem. Nomolaries themselves form patterned cultural plans designed to manage still larger and more abstract aspects of human life. The most abstract and general nomemes reflect the broadest and most desirable human ends. They are concerned with some form of long range security, with the continuance of life and with the meaning of existence. They are the ultimate goals and desires of mankind. Limited in number, and perhaps universal, they are often expressed as general values such as 'honesty', 'compassion', 'love thy neighbor', 'live a long life' or 'strive to be healthy'.

Each of these statements is a general directive and the successful attainment of these major premises is dependent upon the construction of more specific second level nomemes. These nomemes are primarily concerned with understanding and achieving order and regularity in the life processes. At this level a basic proposition might state that understanding the regularity in nature will increase the probability of reaching the ultimate goal. Understanding and working in harmony with nature will enable man to see the recurrent pattern of the seasons, and to prepare for the advent of winter by working hard in the summer and thus improve the chance of surviving.

When order does not naturally exist or cannot be perceived then man must construct it. If natural foods do not occur to satisfy his regularly recurring hunger, then he must create order by growing crops or storing excess foods. He must regulate other activities in his world; conducting relations with people, managing the diversity of man through principles of leadership, communicating through grammar. By creating order through cultural nomemes he will improve his security and his chances for a long life and happiness. The accumulation of wealth, the attainment of power and control, and the maintenance of health, contribute to the greater purpose of attaining the ultimate goals of life.

For example in America a common premise is "work hard and become wealthy." A corollary of this is that "time is money," since there is only so much working time in which to gain the wealth for which one strives. These ideas permeate the whole economic structure. If one man is more efficient with his time, he may make more money and increase his chances of becoming wealthy. If he has more money he has the opportunity to buy more things. The more things he buys the higher prices rise to take advantage of the increased purchasing power. But the man who does not make good use of his time and does not increase his wealth, finds that as the price of goods increases, he can buy less and less, and his whole existence becomes threatened by the fact that the first man makes better use of his time and has more money to spend. Therefore everyone who works on the "Time is money" principle struggles constantly to use his time more effectively so that others will not earn more money than he does and raise the price of goods to the point where he cannot afford them. Corporations take advantage of this principle when they hire salesmen on a commission basis. This concept also favors energetic and aggressive individuals over non-aggressive persons.

The salesman's livelihood depends upon the amount of gross sales he registers and the number of sales represents time since each transaction requires a certain period to consummate. Consequently a car salesman and other persons working on this concept are forced to develop methods of fast sale. The first aspect of the fast sale technique is to learn how to understand the customer; that is, to construct a set of nomemes by which one can distinguish the buyer from the looker, the easy sale from the hard sale.

The salesman sizes up the customer quickly either by his appearance and actions or by his response to some carefully placed questions. On the basis of this first appraisal the salesman selects a sales role which he feels will induce the customer to become a buyer. If it is a little old lady who obviously knows nothing about automobiles, he immediately becomes an expert. To the timid buyer he becomes aggressive and intimidating, to the knowledgeable person he becomes friendly and innocent. If the customer reveals himself to be a looker only then the salesman must quickly get rid of him, for every minute spent with him is a dollar lost. These are some of the nomemes that might derive from the "time is money" principle.

There are innumerable principles of this type in every society: 'Honesty is the best policy', 'treat your neighbor as you wish to be treated', 'expect the best but prepare for the worst.' While not related to any specific situation, the instructions which they contain can be applied to many behavioral episodes to guide the person toward successful management of his life.

Summary

This section has attempted to take the concept of culture out of the category of a vague descriptive device and give it a precise operational meaning. It has been suggested that culture at its simplest operational level consists of the smallest meaningful mental instruction for behavior, and that this unit be called a nomeme. Nomemes are grouped into sequentially arranged orders or nomolaries. Their size, length and complexity are related to the history of the social group and the complexity of the task. It has further been suggested that the creation of nomemes from experience is a fundamental human and animal characteristic.

In the following chapters the implications of this theory of culture will be related to a number of human activities. The purpose is not to repeat well established knowledge but to indicate where the concept of culture fits into a general theory of behavior.

CHAPTER FOUR

THE PURPOSE OF CULTURE

Culture arose out of the evolutionary processes of life, of life forms growing and changing in response to the waxing and waning of the environmental world, of man's continuous struggle to survive. It began as a supplement to the biological limitations of the early man-forms, as an accident of the constant pressure to increase the life potential. It was a response that differed only in kind from the constant biological adaptations occurring throughout the animal world. The natural tools of the first man-forms were meager at best. Lacking claws, fangs, swiftness, or brute strength upon which other animals relied, man needed an alternate strategy in order to compete in life. Without such a development these pre-men, these seemingly helpless creatures, would have stagnated and withered and remained like other animals bound to a simple biological destiny. That they would have survived is possible since many of their relatives have, living in the trees and jungle, arrested at the animal stage. But out of this struggle came far more than mere survival. There emerged a new dimension to life which gradually was to become the dominant mark of man.

As with all living things, man's first task is the continuance of human life. He is always involved with life security, constantly striving to gain or increase it. Situations of insecurity produce behavior and responses aimed at regaining security again. If insecurity persists neither man nor animals can survive. One of the primary ways that man seeks to improve his security is by seeing and understanding the regularities in the existential world and by creating a corresponding regularity in his behavior. Animals, of course, have a similar pattern of behavior and are biologically programmed to make use of regular events, situations, and conditions. Birds expect the air to support them in flight, lions expect zebras to provide meat. Imagine their dismay if the air gave way or the lion found only sawdust.

Man extends his inherent biological mechanisms with a learned system whose success also depends largely on working with regularly occurring problems. New and unique problems can be managed only by making analogies and comparisons with prior situations and solutions. These learned systems work both to solve existing problems and to suppress and discourage new and exceptional problems from arising. Obviously pre-solutions or nomemes cannot exist for problems that have not occurred, and consequently attempts to solve new problems have a high rate of initial failure.

Human life can be viewed as a vast unfolding array of problems. Life is an unending struggle which every person makes to reduce, avoid, or solve his problems. Decision making is the primary activity of man. Problems come in endless multitudes, in countless sizes and shapes, in every conceivable form and degree of consciousness. Many are direct threats to continued existence, but most are neither dramatic nor critical and often go unrecognized. They may entail nothing more serious than deciding how to spend a few spare hours, or what to order in a restaurant, but all must be solved.

Problems originate not only in the external world but in the internal life of the individual as well. They may remain inside and concealed, never rising to the surface level of expression, or they may be obvious, unavoidable, and effect large segments of society.

Problems differ for different societies and different times. They are often only perceived when cultural means for recognition are available. While the problems of one society are not necessarily the problems of the next, there nevertheless are many problems that are so common that all societies have had to struggle to solve them.

As an ongoing biological and chemical organization, every human is constantly involved with securing the basic metabolic requirements of life. Loss of air, water, food, extremes of cold and heat, prolonged wetness, discomfort, exhaustion, inability to get sleep, wounds, illnesses all generate problem solving reactions. Even when the metabolic needs are cared for, other dangers are never far. Droughts, floods, fire, and physical calamities are a constant threat. Early man found that bacillae, parasites, insects, reptiles, and ferocious beasts existed everywhere. They presented constant problems. If man was going to solve them and survive, he had to develop powerful tools. The human potential for enjoying life and securing happiness must wait, art and music can come only after there is some guarantee of life. This assurance may only be momentary, a few seconds or minutes, or it may be relatively permanent. Gradually through time man increased the periods of security available until today vast numbers of people live and die without experiencing anything more difficult in their lives than minor inconvenience.

While the primary problem of human life is simply coping with the environment and the biological requirements of life, far more human problems are created by man himself. These occur as a result of the need to cooperate with other people in a mutually advantageous way. There are problems of where one belongs in society, of status and roles, of getting along with other groups of men, of conflicts and wars. There are the problems of what to do about the unknowns and unsolvables of life, of understanding oneself, of malfunctions in the social machinery, of loss of esteem, of anger from others, of inability to succeed.

Essentially man faces all impinging problems in one of two ways, either individually and alone, or in the company of others. The discovery that cooperative behavior produced a much higher success rate than individual effort occurred far back in time before true man arose. Although man is by no means the only gregarious animal, the development of a high order of mutual sharing has been the key factor in human history. It is through this sharing that man became human. This sharing of behavioral experiences led to the standardization of behavior within human groups and it is this standardization and not behavior itself that provides the clue to understanding human life. Why do members of a social group act in such similar ways? Why do their tools and material objects come in standardized shapes and sizes? Why does a person respond to the same or similar problems in a habitual manner? Simply to say that culture is responsible is meaningless unless the mechanisms of its operation are made explicit.

The advantages of cooperation are many. Primarily they derive from the potential of multiple experience to provide more avenues for solving problems than individual and isolated experience. But only if the experience can be accumulated and shared in some usable form. Man is at least partially equal to the task of turning experience into usable form and he has carried the usefulness of group experience to heights far beyond the achievements of other animals. The raw material for culture development is forged in cooperative behavior and conversely culture is the expression of group cooperation.

While individually man is relatively ineffectual, he is not totally helpless. He comes into life with a number of tools: with biological responses, with behavioral characteristics, with human capabilities. The infant reacts to colors, to brightness, to loud or sudden noise, to rhythmic sounds, to movements, odors, and to irregularities. Bright lights, spots, glints, all attract his eye. Moving objects get his attention. Many animals have these responses; man has more.

He is curious, investigative, persistent, and energetic. He seeks explanations. Objects and events within his life space are subject to his curiosity. He pokes and pries, tears apart, and puts together. He has the capacity to create new things, to make new objects from old things, to manufacture things that never existed before. He has the ability to enjoy, to have pleasure. But he can also become bored and he easily alternates between satisfying his needs and being satisfied.

With this array of tools man went about subduing the formidable phalanx of demands and problems that pressed upon him. For thousands and hundreds of thousands of years, he struggled. Over and over again these problems reappeared in new dress, camouflaged by the immediateness and the uniqueness of each particular historic situation. But some men solved each of them sufficiently to survive and multiply. They survived by accumulating the individual solutions made through time, by abstracting them into usable nomemes and eventually provided themselves with a vastly more acute and flexible survival tool than was available through their genetic or biological equipment alone. Today every individual arrives in an existing cultural world just as he inherits the atmosphere. If this were not so, if this cultural order did not exist, each person would face an overwhelming task for he would have to learn by himself all the facts and rules necessary for survival without help from others, without tools, language, social structure, or knowledge. Without the existence of an accumulated body of cultural materials from which the individual can draw, each person would have to begin at the beginning. It is unlikely he would survive the first serious situation which confronted him, because he would not be able to make an effective tool, or find food, or get along with other people. His knowledge would be limited to his own immediate experience, and his behavior would be chaotic and based primarily on direct, innate response to stimuli. But this is not the case and he does not have to learn everything from direct personal experience.

Human existence is characterized by a completely different and more powerful technique for dealing with life. It is no longer necessary for each person to spend a lifetime merely learning how to survive. By relying on ready-made nomemes, man can avoid errors and disastrous detours and begin to utilize his experiences in more meaningful and human ways. He can grow through his own unique personal experience as well as through the accumulated history of others; and even more, he can benefit from the immediate shared activities of his group so that he can accomplish things that alone would be far beyond his capabilities.

Every individual begins at birth recreating in his mind the nomemes of his culture which he learns to apply to specific problems. These problems generally require some kind of resolution before the individual can continue his life journey, and the nature of the resolution is largely dependent upon the body of existing nomolaries available.

As a decision maker in solving common problems man has developed numerous universal patterns of behavior. He has everywhere created a technological culture, a world of material physical objects. These tools, roads, bridges, machines, houses, pots and pans, are his means of dealing with certain aspects of the physical universe. Man everywhere has methods of obtaining, transporting and consuming food, clothing, and other necessities. He has developed elaborate systems of nomemes regarding the division of labor, the utilization of specialized skills, of ownership, use, and inheritance of property. Complex and elaborate nomemes have been devised to handle the problems of social order, of marriage, of kinship, of institutions, and of the rights and privileges of individuals. Most societies have formal techniques for providing each person with a social slot, a status, and a role. All cultures have methods of moving a person through the life crisis events of birth, puberty, marriage, and death. These are not left to chance, to the capacity of the individual to handle.

Even the deeply personal problems of the meaning of

life, fate, and the explanation of death have their cultural answers. Questions of good and bad, right and wrong, joy and pleasure, arise in every society, and are dealt with in cultural ways. Each society has provided pathways for deviancy, for satisfactions in life, techniques for maintaining psychic equilibrium, for reducing anxiety and despair. All of these cultural manifestations are integrated into a system, a dynamic interacting plan. The links in this integrated structure are tied in such a way that alterations and changes in one are apt to affect all.

The cultural nomemes developed by any particular society can take any shape which can withstand the test of survival. Just as many different kinds of games can be invented, so many different kinds of cultures have come into being. They are not totally arbitrary, however, since they are subject to the currents of history and the opportunities and requirements presented by the environmental and social setting which they occupy. Thus a set of nomemes may provide elaborate means for enhancing goodwill and positive interrelationships among the members of a society or it may encourage hostility, hate and frequent fighting. The Hopi and Zumi emphasize reasonable in-group harmony. They strongly de-emphasize certain kinds of individualism, aggressiveness, ambition, and self-centered behavior. They may even take serious actions against people who demonstrate these traits for they are perceived as disrupting the smooth flow of pueblo life.

On the other hand, events on the Great Plains during the last century required another kind of man, an individual who could face danger, risk, and death. But all this was for a purpose. The Plains were in turmoil and in flux. Danger to the group and to the individual lurked on every side. A man had to be ready and able to protect his family and his neighbors. Fear, doubt, or hesitation in the face of attack were death knells. But no man really wanted to die by sacrificing himself in foolish demonstrations of bravado. Bravery and aggressiveness were attributes which society rewarded in men who took the risk, who had the appearance of disdain for death, who were brave and ferocious because the society needed these kinds of men in order to survive. Warriors would, through the rewards of social approval, ritual, music, and dances, build themselves up to facing certain death, while in fact proclaiming a desire to die fighting.

In parts of New Guinea, men are fearful, hostile, treacherous and dangerous. They develop children with the same qualities who are capable of standing the stresses produced by a hostile environment. Softness, kindness, consideration for others would only be regarded as signs of weakness and fear. They would bring sure extinction as a tribe.

All these are self-preservation techniques developed by the society in its life course. They are not the product of some innate need for aggression, anger, hate, or love. Rather they are a response to a reality situation, a situation that is not always easy to ascertain. The society creates out of its culture and its history the kinds of individuals it needs for continued survival. If it does not, it becomes an historic artifact.

Culture then must be seen as a functional device, a tool which seeks to increase the utility of the life experience both for the individual and the group. But the way it does this is not necessarily direct or obvious. While its raw materials are individual experiences, its finished product is abstracted, summarized, and organized in such a way that the experience is often unrecognizable. Nevertheless these materials are capable of being recalled, compared, and appropriately used as models for behavior. Behavior may be dependent upon the arousal of emotional states in subtle ways, through attachments to the familiar, or upon special skills or knowledge. It may be dependent upon no individual but upon group organization, in cooperation and distribution of leadership and member roles.

In a fundamental way culture is an attempt to order the chaos of existence. Chaos is created by hunger, cold, thirst, or by many things happening at once. It is children being born while others die, or illness that comes for no reason, or lightning that strikes one and not another. Ordering the chaos of existence involves finding and recognizing the regularities of nature and putting these into a comprehensive world picture. The crisis points in the environmental world, winter cold, summer drought, floods and storms, are treated as recurring phenomena which can be anticipated and for which preparations can be made. The life cycle events of birth, puberty, marriage, pregnancy, death are marked so that social support is provided during these periods of individual stress.

Man also attempts to control the future by clarifying the alternatives in choice situations. By developing nomemes that produce preferred forms of behavior, culture effectively binds and guides individuals and society through periods of confusion and indecision. By striving to reduce the number of alternatives at problem crossroads, psychic energy otherwise expended in making routine decisions is conserved. Inability to resolve a problem often produces increasingly greater emotional response and decreasing rational effort in human beings. All problem solving involves some emotional commitment, the intensity of which is related to the perceived seriousness of the situation and the availability of a solution. Culture helps to reduce anxiety produced by the necessity of making decisions where insufficient means are available.

Anxiety is a product of uncertainty about the future and about the choice one must make in solving a situational or life problem. It arises when an individual comes to a problem and must make a decision but has no adequate guides to follow. It is one of the tasks of culture to provide the guides either with the specific nomemes or by a prior elimination of the alternatives. Culture reduces the multitude of responses available for each problem by providing proven behavioral nomemes that direct action to satisfactory conclusions. These presolutions increase the probability of individual and social survival and reduce the interpersonal and intrapersonal potential for quarrels.

It is obvious that not all problems are solvable in an immediate or direct manner and that everyone is subject to a certain amount of anxiety and frustration. But an excess of anxiety or frustration can be damaging and dangerous since it may immobilize the individual or fix his attention upon one problem to the exclusion of others which are even more threatening. The inability to resolve problems can therefore become self-destructive. Consequently, all societies have explicit instructions for solving the problems its members will encounter, but they also have mechanisms aimed at preventing the occurrence of unsolvable problems or of what to do when unsolvable problems arise. These may take the form of avoidance through withdrawal into conditions of psychological helplessness, if necessary, or the development of a ceremony of release where the emotional energies associated with anxieties and frustrations can be vented into another prescribed direction. The joking relationships between prescribed members of the group, gossip, or witchcraft are mechanisms of this sort available in different societies. Under certain situations a person can say or do things normally prohibited but which permits him to redirect his emotions into harmless behavior.

Man not only creates guides for present and future behavior, he goes beyond that. He creates the future. He does not sit passively waiting for events to happen. Because he constructs presolution nomemes to guide his activity he comes to expect these occurrences and to be ready for them. Because he has planned in advance, occurrences are directed into certain controlled channels. He thus constructs a predictability which extends far beyond merely being ready with certain prescribed reactions. He sets up a pattern of behavior which shapes the future. Such predictability is essential for any complex form of social life. Complementary and noncomplementary activity must dovetail in order to be effective. Driving an automobile in heavy traffic not only depends upon the predictability of all the drivers but obviously it depends upon the construction of roads, bridges, and signals, all built in anticipation that people will use them in prescribed ways.

Culture thus functions to order the structure of the society as well as the life of the individual. The individual achieves his existence through the existence of other individuals who share a part of his life and through the fact that most human activity stems from interaction with other people. This interaction is mediated by the social structure and the cultural nomemes. Thus the individual is bound to his society since if he wishes to speak he must use an understandable language, if he wishes to act, his acts must be in a comprehensible form to which there can be a corresponding response. The only place he can secure this response is from people who share his language and other cultural assets. It is apparent that while culture is a product of human association, it functions to bind people together into the very groupness that sustains it. It does this through the nomemes of language, kinship structure, family, marriage, social organization, economics, art, and religion.

This binding characteristic exists as a bond to the past as well as to the present. The historic bond is represented by the behavior of older people who are acting out of nomemes they learned in an earlier time. It is carried on by buildings and roads and social structures that persist from generation to generation. Nevertheless, at any given point in time the social-cultural system must function in a contemporary context. It must deal with current situations and with the new generation. Thus in both vertical and horizontal dimensions the individual is bound into the cultural system.

Man exists as a human being only in the context of society and culture. For man to survive even as an animal he must be a member of a group. The social order provides the necessary structure for man to survive and men everywhere live in groups. These groups have organization and behavioral nomemes which themselves become goals and rewards. Culture is man's ultimate reward.

CHAPTER FIVE

BEHAVING, CULTURE AND NOMEMES

All organisms are behaving even when it is not apparent and all behavior has some guiding system that shapes it. To live is to behave, but behavior is never spontaneous and arbitrary. It is always caused, with a purpose and meaning, a beginning and an ending. It is a response to some reality situation and some necessity.

Human behavior is no more arbitrary than the activity of other animals. It does not just occur, just happen, just flow out of the unlimited vitality of the individual. Like other behavior it is shaped and guided, but includes a far greater learned factor than is present in most animal behavior. While all human behavior is not cultural, most human activity is influenced by culture.

Human activity is not a product of any single factor but the result of the interaction of biological, cultural, and personal elements which are fused into a single guidance system. This guidance system is set in motion by other forces, by activity occurring in the external world, by the demands and requirements that arise in the internal physiological structure of the body, and from the memory system. In every human, culture and biology are interwoven into a vast and complex fabric, woof and warp, color and pattern, without separation, stitched on the loom of each person's life.

Animals, like man, act in a real world, a world full of randomness, of the unexpected and accidental. Many acts of nature appear arbitrary, spontaneous and unpredictable; rainstorms, earthquakes, eruptions, floods, fires, thunder, lightning, injuries, and death. On the other hand, other events are regular and predictable; the appearance of hunger, thirst, day and night, predators in the evening, the sounds and movements of other animals. The ability to perceive randomness or regularity varies widely for different animals, but for most, the world is made up of two classes of events, those that they can perceive as random and unpredictable, and those which they see as regular and ordered. All animals must adjust their life style to these two conditions in some manner.

Animals can make greater use of regularity than they can of randomness. Events that occur at a regular time or place become expected. The animal that can grasp the regularity in various situations and can adjust his behavior to take advantage of these occurrences improves his chances of survival. Consequently, many, if not all, animals have evolved systems for recognizing and anticipating some order in the world around them. If they lacked this capacity they would be unable to learn from experience. The ability to recognize and project regularity upon the apparent randomness of the world is fundamental to both animal and human behavior and basic to the concept of culture.

All animals are born with some unlearned capacity to act, however slight and however indeterminate. They will display this capacity without prior experience. This innate system was given to them on the basis of certain long range regularities in the total environment and in the expected life pattern of the organism. It is a system developed out of the life experiences of generations of the species, out of the selection and survival potentials of millions of behavior acts. Drop by drop they have been distilled into a residual of automatic responses and predispositions.

This behavioral residual, these innate factors, are passed on from parent to offspring much as are arms, legs, claws, hooves and hair. They are concerned with basic functions, with the operation of the biological system. They regulate the heart beat, breathing, defecation, body temperature, and metabolism. These activities have regularity and predictability. They have the appearance of rhythms, with regular alternations of activity and non-activity. Many are reactive like hunger and eating, thirst and drinking, fatigue and sleeping. This regularity is not accidental; it is closely related to environmental activities such as the alternation of night and day, the rotation of the months and years, birth and death, exhaustion and restoration.

Regularity is further produced by the nature of the organism itself. The body is limited in the amount of metabolic necessities it can absorb at any given time. It can take in only so much food, water or air. These materials are consumed at a fairly constant rate and they must be replenished on a regular basis. They are so fundamental and critical that their acquisition is not left to volition, but is genetically coded. Their needs occur automatically and insistently. But they are obvious. Other rhythms are not so apparent--alternations in feeling states, moods, fatigue, excitement, and depression. The regularities in these activities are harder to measure, more difficult to detect. Nevertheless they are there.

The unlearned dispositions of animals exist because certain regularities in the world have been anticipated and prepared for. Corresponding behavior is programmed into the animal. So long as regularly anticipated events occur in the life space of the programmed animal, he can begin life without having to learn everything through his own trial and error efforts. But because the universe is also full of the unexpected and the random each organism needs and develops another more flexible guidance mechanism. It develops this system from its experience in life, gradually merging its life experience with the system which it inherits. The degree to which various animals can develop and take advantage of their learned nomemic systems varies greatly. It depends upon the species, the kinds of experiences it is subject to and the complexity of its natural development. This capacity in humans is called intelligence, and is measured by displays of insight and of problem solving ability. But varying degrees of insight, problem solving ability, and tool usage are found throughout the animal world. Seldom can they be separated into clear categories of innate or learned behavior.

The totality of behavior and activity is the joint result of learned factors overlaying the biological as individuals cope with their existence. This nomemic system does not develop without structure. On the contrary, it is framed by the larger regularities and rhythms of life. The particular life pattern of each species is paramount. Although each species has a general life style, these are flexible and there is a range of appropriate behavior within each stage of the life cycle. Within this frame, the development of the nomemic system is basically a personal matter for each animal.

But humans are different. Through the endless changes of evolution they have developed a special kind of guidance system, a system that makes far greater use of the shared experience of individuals. It is dependent upon the greater facility human beings have to accumulate and exchange information from generation to generation. Non-human animals are very limited in their ability to share experience or to pass it on from parent to offspring. Humans with their superior memory and communication ability have created a new world, a new system that is far more flexible and responsive to immediate life situations. They have created the cultural system.

Culture vastly increases the volume of behavioral nomemes available to any individual. While the genetic code provides basic metabolic and structural principles, culture elaborates these principles endlessly.

Culture is dependent upon memory, upon the ability to store, organize and recall not only vast amounts of information, but useful and instant answers to pressing problems. It does little good for a man to have acquired massive data and rules regarding what to do on meeting a tiger if they are not usable during a face to face encounter. If the mind functions too slowly or incorrectly it negates its advantages. Where death is a constant threat, survival is dependent upon instantaneous recall of the proper reactions; it is here that the organization of memory is crucial. Lower animals have simple memories. The higher animals, the primates in particular, have complex memories. They store a vastly increased mass of material but they also have a greater range of experience to manipulate.

In the evolution of man, individuals whose memories did not contribute to their survival fell by the wayside. Those who benefited passed on the residual of their life experience to their offspring. These residuals were in the form of simple nomemes and instructions which were reinforced by constant use. In man, memory not only became highly developed in itself but was supported by elaborate cultural techniques of organization and ritual. Thus, while culture is dependent upon memory, it in turn functions to improve the quality of memory.

Numerous analogies to human behavior occur among other animals, and man shares many of the same physiological properties and rhythms found in far simpler organisms. But he is the only creature to have created a behavior-determining device as pervasive as culture and this potential for culture appears to be a biological characteristic of the species. Man is unique because he has an extended ability to generalize and to abstract. He can see the relationships among a wider range of variables than other animals. He has a greater symbolizing ability. He can visualize in his mind things and events that are not immediately present. He can give things names, and then manipulate the name. He has a greater ability for self-observation and self-awareness than other animals. While other complex animals have these qualities to some degree and can generalize or recognize the similarity between like objects, this ability is generally far less developed than in humans. Often they are limited by the sensory instruments they possess, by the sharpness or vagueness of their discrimination capability.

Many animals also symbolize, at least in a rudimentary way. They can retain key clues in a memory system by which they can recognize objects and classes of things from one experience to the next. They develop mental images which can be compared with immediately perceived objects. If they did not have this ability it would be impossible for them to equate what they saw yesterday with what they see today, and in this sense the stored memory image is a symbol of the actual object.

Animals self observe just as man does. They distinguish between themselves and other animals, between themselves and natural objects. They know when they are threatened, when they are injured and hurt. The difference is one of degree. Even though chimpanzees can recognize themselves in mirrors, may prance and primp, they hardly know what to make of what they see. Man on the other hand can develop not only a concept of his physical self, but also an image of what he is like as an experiencing being. He can observe his own mistakes and self correct by altering his behavior in line with the image he wishes to project. These qualities are indispensible to human life. They are an integrated part of man's behavior. This ability to conceptualize an object or symbolize an event beyond its immediate presences is critical to the emergence of culture. Symbolic tools, sounds, movements, and gestures transform individual experience into culturally meaningful codes. Even such a simple thing as naming has vast implications. It is the beginning of communication, of the transference of knowledge. Without this quality human behavior would be extremely limited. It would consist primarily of reactive responses, imitation, or reenactment.

Like other animals, man has the innate ability to see relationships and similarities and to form categories. This is a basic animal characteristic since even simple primates can realize when two events are alike. Monkeys can learn by trial and error which involves the capacity to distinguish between two classes of events, success and failure. A small child learns that a door is to be closed by observing adults. Despite the fact that there may be many kinds of doors, in many shapes, sizes, and colors, the child will dutifully run about shutting all of them. Somehow he has been able to generalize and see a relationship among a variety of doors. The child quickly develops a nomeme that doors are to be shut. Even though this applied in the beginning to only one door he soon extends this to all doors through his ability to recognize that doors are a class of objects.

The function of any nomeme is dependent upon the recognition of the category to which it applies. A category always includes a range of concepts and is seldom a single entity. There are always particular examples of the category which are peripheral in that they contain as few of the characteristics of the category as possible while still remaining within the class. Red fades off into pink or orange or purple but it is never easy to say where these other colors begin and red ends, or how far one should apply the nomemes that pertains to red. The generalizing capacity of man enables him to see the regularity and order necessary for human life and to apply appropriate nomemes.

Experiences and responses to experiences also can be categorized into different dimensions. The category of experience influences the kind of behavioral response that results. At one level all experience and behavior is personal and individual, unique and private, unlike anyone else's. It happens only to that particular unit of life known as the person. It never happens to any-one else in the same way. It can only be shared vicariously, and it is not dependent upon the actions of others. It develops out of the particular body struc-ture, the life situations, and the biological properties of a particular individual.

But other experiential situations and the behavior associated with those events are more than personal.

They are common and are shared by many people. Everyone gets hungry and eats, wears clothes, sleeps at night, laughs, cries, feels happy or depressed. Many people are exposed to the same kind of event and react in much the same way. They all recognize the experience and the behavior. They know what it means and how it feels. At least in a general way they can share both the experience and the responses with others because it has also happened to them.

There is yet another kind of experience and corresponding behavior. It is different from the others because it is more than shared, and is dependent upon other people, upon interaction among one or more persons. Marriage, group games, political activity, law, and war are experiences made possible only as a group effort.

Probably little behavior is so totally personal that it is in fact unique. The uniqueness is minor, in small things, in variations of common experiences. Learning to walk, being hungry, cold, fearful--these are common behaviors but each has an element of the unique and personal.

Behavior can be described as culturally modifiable or culturally dependent. While hunger is a purely personal experience, the particular time one eats or what one eats or how one eats to gratify hunger is subject to modification by cultural forces. Every man develops hunger pangs but satisfying his hunger is usually dependent on a series of interrelated behaviors which determine what foods are available, how they will be prepared, when and how they will be eaten.

A second type of activity is entirely culturally dependent and cannot exist outside the cultural context. This includes such behavior as speaking, courtship, political activity, marriage, most ritual social organization, games, and war. The only way these events or activities can occur at all is if there are other people involved who are using similar nomemes.

To summarize, each individual is bound into biocultural structures that are universal and inevitable.

The most pervasive of these are the physiological system and the life pattern. All persons pass through a series of chronological ordered biological stages in the course of their existence. These include birth, infancy, childhood, adolescence, adulthood, old age, and death. The life span has a pattern of growing and declining which is shared by everyone. Developing around these biological factors, man has constructed a non-biological system that gives him flexibility and a capacity to manage life problems far beyond a simple genetic response.

All creatures have guidance systems combining in various proportions the innate qualities they possess with the learned experiences of life. In man these learned experiences have largely dominated the biological components of existence or made them more effective. Culture is the group expression of what man has learned from experience and is expressed through behavioral nomemes.

CHAPTER SIX

WHERE BEHAVIOR BEGINS

Behavior begins in the brain, swiftly, silently, unseen. The brain is a generator, a factory. Its product is activity. It takes raw materials from the environment and from its own resources, puts them through the machinery of the mind and transforms them into articles of behavior. The processes are dependent upon each other; what goes in affects what occurs and what emerges. But the brain is not simply a passive, listless engine waiting to be switched on, or stimulated and motivated into action. It is constructed to seek out, locate, and secure the items needed to create behavior. It feeds upon sensory materials. Deprived of these goods, it can lose the capacity to operate and produce effective behavior. It will stagnate, atrophy, and die.

Culture is a product of the organization and functional capacity of the human brain. It is not something separate, distinct, existing in isolation from other behavior. Conversely, the human brain has responded to and been influenced by the needs and demands of culture. With each step in the evolutionary growth of man, the brain became steadily larger and more effective. It increased its ability to secure data, to organize and store experience, to detect relationships among many bits of information, to profit from its own mistakes.

Massive and complex, the human brain grew into a highly integrated mechanism composed of sensory tools, storage bins, and activators, all joined in intricate networks structured to function in unison and directed toward the production of a single commodity, the behavioral nomemes which would guide the organism's activity.

Most significantly the human brain developed a very special characteristic which appears to be directly connected with the ability to construct nomemes. The cerebral surface is divided into two hemispheres and each hemisphere has developed special cognitive abilities. The right hemisphere in most humans appears to have responsibility for standard cognitive processes of processing spatial configuration, objects, and relationships. The left hemisphere, on the other hand, developed a unique capacity to use symbols and to manipulate, order, and re-arrange them into logical sequences. This capacity to manipulate symbols is directly related to the ability to perceive situations and to construct plans and strategies to solve problems.

Many processes within the brain are themselves molded and shaped by culture. Learned nomemes of perception and response are inserted into the basic production flow. Consequently, culture is more than a passive product, a merchandise turned out mechanically by the brain. It enters into the very processes themselves, into the full range of mental activity. It is critical in decision making, especially in the crucial process of selecting the appropriate behavior nomemes. It is even more apparent in activating behavior itself.

The human infant does not come into the world totally naked and unprepared, a clean parchment upon which his life will be etched. If this were so, he would remain unwritten upon. Rather, he already has many capabilities. These will enable him to experience and to respond under the proper circumstances to the world around him. He will use his legs to walk, his hands to finger, his ears to hear, his tongue to taste, his

vocal cords to sound, his brain to conduct its fundamental processes. These attributes come with certain
expectations about the world. When only a few days
old, his eyes can differentiate movement from non-
movement, recognizing whether things are directed
toward him or away. He can tell that objects seen can
also be touched; and that they have shape and solidity.
Sounds attract not only his ears but his eyes, for
sounds come from things, and things are located in
space. Objects that disappear are nevertheless somewhere and movements of things are already anticipated
by the infant even when he has never seen them before.
Helpless and untutored as the newborn appears, he
comes armed with a brain already organized to make
sense from his first encounter with the external world.
More than that, he is able to use his first experience
as a tool by which to manage future experiences.
Minimal as these features are initially, they are the
foundation upon which, little by little, the infant grows
and becomes a man. Not too much at first nor all at
once, but step by step and stage by stage, the hidden
capacities unfold themselves in the maturing of the
growing child.

As the experiential world grows and develops, as
the hand becomes handy, the legs capable of walking,
the tongue and lips begin to shape words, words arise
to accommodate the voice, tools the hands, and brains
the creature.

So the cultural person comes into existence as the
biology of the body fashions knowledge and experience
into the pattern of man's being. Layer upon layer of
experience forms like a pearl around the life-core until
he emerges with a unique meaningful self, a selfbeing
capable of actualizing his experience in a manner as
closely approximating freedom and choice as man will
ever reach.

The behavior-producing processes are not clearly
or fully understood. They are complex, immense, and
concealed. Nevertheless, the flow can be deduced and
its sequential steps can be outlined in a general way.
Like a train whizzing through stations and suburbs.

the load of raw perceptions is rushed from broad awareness to selective awareness. Quickly, the perception unit is shuttled to identification, comparison, recognition, and categorization. Transformed into thought units, some are stored, others are sent on for immediate potency evaluation and use in decision making. They are rushed to production, pushed into molds and models and transformed into behavioral nomemes, finally to emerge in action as movements of the arms, hands, legs, body, tongue, or eyes.

The cognitive ability of animals is marked by different levels congruent with their different evolutionary stages. With the simplest animals there is merely a passive receptivity of external signals. Reception of the signal triggers a direct and automatic response in the organism. Even these creatures make distinctions between various types of excitation and thus categorize reality in a rudimentary way. Further development leads to a recognition of sensory material as objects existing in a spatial dimension. It becomes possible to distinguish between various kinds of objects. The animal is no longer limited to gross awareness of simple sights, sounds, or smells. As sensory discrimination increases there is a realization that some objects which can be sensorally separated have activity. They affect each other and can be affected.

Still greater understanding of the world is obtained when the organism realizes that the objects he perceives can be grouped and categorized into units. He can recognize the quality of likeness between objects. This capacity is directly related to the ability to form mental images and to retain these images in memory. Identification and classification grow out of the brain's increasing ability to transfer sensory images into memory images. A sensory image is closer to the memory unit. A much more advanced stage of cognitive ability is reached when an arbitrary model can be substituted for the image model. The use of the arbitrary or abstract model increases the ability of the mind to deal with more complex concepts. The highest stage of cognitive ability occurs when several arbitrary models are synthesized into abstract concepts devoid of any immediate references to real events existing in the world. Concepts are derived from experience but humans can construct concepts indirectly. They can imagine ghosts although no one has ever seen one.

In the simple animals there is a direct excitation-reaction quality to behavior. In humans there are many intermediate steps between the sensory material and the behavioral result. Simple stimulus reaction has evolved into a train of excitation, effect, memory, identification, association, and behavior.

A complex animal gathers materials useful in the construction of behavior in three ways: from the external world, from his internal organs, and from his memory. A predator may appear in the visual landscape, hunger pangs churn the stomach, or one may recall some previous event. Hunger, thirst, internal pain, sexual pressure are sources of behavior. They do not pass through the external receptors but are relayed directly to recognition areas. Memory activation also bypasses the external senses although, again, external events may initiate recall.

The brain is alert, responsive, and active in seeking information about the world and about the organism of which it is a part. It gathers many kinds of sensory data. It can process information from one or more receptors if the signals are regular or predictable but normally sensory material must be treated in serial order to prevent interference and confusion.

The gathering of behavioral materials is the function of the eyes, ears, tongue, nose, and skin. These organs take the raw material they get from the external world, transform them into sensory data and transmit this data on to specialized areas of the brain. The capacity of each sense is limited. Each is bound to a particular segment of the sensory world; to light, sound, taste, touch, heat, balance, pressure, and cold. They are specific in that the nose does not hear, the ear does not see. They are open to a vast amount of information, but some give more data than others. If one smells a sharp odor, that is all he knows. He cannot deduce the size, shape, color, or taste of the smell. But to see a color is also to see the object that is colored, and that is to know its size and its shape. To feel with one's hand an object tells us something about its texture and size, but not its color or smell. To perceive heat tells us nothing about color.

The sensory capacity is inherent. But the threshold levels can be altered by experience and training. All the sensory instruments do is gather raw data. The signals they receive mean little before they are pro- cessed by the brain. They are merely light, sound, or odors connected with nothing. The world is full of such signals. Sounds strike the ear constantly; the noise of wind blowing, cars roaring by, people talking, all occurring at the same time. The air is full of smells; food cooking, gasoline fumes, perfumes and stenches. The day is overflowing with stimuli to one's senses; the texture of concrete and grass, the move- ments of clouds, the warmth of sunshine, the cacoph- ony of sounds both natural and manmade, the scent of flowers, sea, or oil refineries. The brain must make sense and order of this apparent chaos.

The first task in information gathering is to focus awareness on one channel, on noise or sight or sound. Each major sensor is capable of distinguishing specific aspects of the total signal. Light can be resolved into various colors, sounds into high or low, tastes into sweet or bitter. The incoming material goes to the brain stem and to a routing system that decides what information to send on and where to send it. Decisions are made--colors, phonemes, smells--each has to be sent to its proper area. The change from gross focus to fine focus occurs here. Fine focus not only con- centrates attention on one kind of data but begins to resolve the data into its component parts. The land- scape is scanned and each object, odor or sound identified as a tree, rock, horse, cloud, coffee, animal, or bird.

For example, a creature identifies one object as food and another as a stone in two ways. A direct comparison can be made between the immediate object and some other external reference, or a comparison can be made between the object and an internal model which has already been stored in the brain. A lion sights another animal in its visual landscape. He must decide whether it is a food animal or another predator. If a previously identified zebra is within view, a direct comparison might be made. If there is no external reference available the lion must make comparisons with memory models of various animals until he has matched the visual object.

The accuracy and discriminatory capacity of these two methods differ. Using direct comparison, the human eye can detect minute differences in brightness, the ear hears frequency difference of only a few cycles per-second. Using indirect comparisons the memory is much less capable of distinguishing small differences in odor, brightness, or tone.

Indirect identification depends upon the animal's capacity to develop through experience a vast series of image models in its memory. All or most of the objects and activities found in the landscape must be catalogued. These identifying models cannot be generalized, cannot simply be zebra or bird or rock. They must note specific characteristics of size, shape, color, movement, odor, sound, location, number, and probably many others. The eye focuses on basic identifying marks, lines, angles, spots, corners, and distances between lines. The evaluation of each of these qualities is dependent upon a measurement and comparison capacity developed within the brain of complex animals. Animals measure relative size, differences in weight, heights, and length of canines. Furthermore, the animal knows what these mean. If they lacked this capacity, we would find cats attacking deer, lions chasing mice, horses running from rabbits.

Each sensor is responsible for a certain kind of evaluation. Sight is concerned with measuring size, shape, color, movement, closeness, and distance. The ear measures loudness, deepness, shrillness, volume, and distances. Appropriate models for each of these characteristics exist in the brain, built up through an interaction of genetic capacities and actual experience. A lion would be thoroughly baffled if an elephant were painted in zebra stripes and turned loose on the veldt for he would be unable to fit the experience with any comparison model he possessed.

Basic and critical in the information processing chain is the capacity for storage and recall of experience. Recognition, categorization, and comparison are dependent on recall capacity. All information storage is not the same however, since distinctions can be made as to the length of time data is stored or held. Obviously not all data is of equal importance nor can all information be held without creating an overload.

A great amount of sensory data is held only momentarily, some to be moved on and stored for short periods of time, the remainder to be discarded. The human visual channel can hold a dozen sight units for a second or two. If the brain focuses on this information, the material may be transferred to a relatively permanent state where it may be stored for the rest of the person's life.

It is unlikely that a single central memory exists, for memory seems to be associated with each sensory organ which automatically provides a means for categorizing data. Nor is the memory image a single unit which can be transferred willy nilly through the brain. Transfer models are developed from master memory images and these are recalled and shuttled about during the brain processes.

When the incoming materials, the information received by the organism, leaves the thalamus or routing system it passes through an affect activator or selector. This affect charge often gives the impression that behavior is largely spontaneous and emotional. Lions snarl, roar and charge, monkeys and apes scream, pound their chests, bare their teeth, dogs bark and snap. But emotions are not that simple. In humans an evaluation process takes place as the information is relayed to the special cortical areas. This acts as a balance or governor on unbridled emotional energies. It integrates the emotional components with data from memory and produces behavior tempered by experience from a broader context.

Each bit of incoming information is measured for its emotional potential; fear, anger, hate, love, joy, or sorrow. It is this step that determines the force or potency of the behavior, assigning it an emotional quotient. It enables different levels of response to be made. All reactions would otherwise have the same intensity whether it was seeing a lion a hundred yards away or on one's doorstep.

This emotional potential or quotient is not a single entity, however, but a relative quality. It is dependent upon the cortical control the animal has and the kinds of experiences it has stored. It may range from little or no fear to complete terror, from mild annoyance to raging anger.

Exchange networks exist between some of the various areas of the brain. If one runs his hand over a ball, one can visualize its shape as if one were looking at it. Lower primates seem to be deficient in some of these connecting networks and children and some adults may not have all of them fully developed. Separate regions in the cortex are responsible for different sensory functions, but there is a great individual variation in the degree of information exchange among these areas. These foci are merely general regions where all related aspects of a sensory modality are lodged. Attached to each foci are integrating areas which contain the memory units as well. The specialized sensory areas are not directly connected with each other. The information they each process goes to their integrating area and this area receives information from the other integration areas. In humans, then, there is an association area in conjunction with each sensory area. Each association area is connected to other specific sense areas. The degree to which the association areas are inter-connected is related to the total evolutionary development of the species and is most extensive in man. Other animals apparently do not have the neural mechanisms for the complex associations found in man. To further complicate the picture of the mental processes, the human brain has developed unique specializations within the cortical areas of each hemisphere or half of the brain. Like the dual nature of many of the sensory organs and of the body structures, the brain also has a dual component in which each half of the brain is specialized in processing certain kinds of behavior.

A remarkable feature of information processing is the capacity animals have for recognizing the similarities among various objects and events and to form categorical groups or patterns based on perceived likenesses. This generalizing-analogy ability is an extension of the categorizing capacity and is closely related to memory. It means that not only is all incoming information examined for exact fit with existing comparison models, but in a new situation or with information that is slightly different, a decision can be made by analogous comparison. In other words, if an object or situation is different from any existing categories an attempt will be made to fit the material to the closest model already held.

The fact that light which strikes the eye becomes sight in the brain is only the beginning of behavior. The eye does not exist merely to gather light and create sight but to assist the animal to produce behavior. Behavior is usually concerned with solving problems. The problem may be eating, mating, running from danger, or attacking a threat. The initial problem is identifying the various objects in the landscape and perhaps focusing on one. Before any overt action can occur all the preliminary steps must take place in the proper sequential order. This insures that the action which is to follow is appropriate to the situation. In most cases an appropriate action model or nomeme already exists as a presolution plan held in another area of memory storage. This can be a program designated as a genetically fixed action pattern or a learned pattern, but it more likely is a combination of both. This is what is called culture.

All behavior is a response to a situation. This situation is either a repeat of an event previously encountered, an event somewhat like a previous situation, or one unlike previous situations. The selected behavior nomemes takes several shapes. For an old situation, the behavior is usually an old response. Even if the individual exercises choice and decides on a new response, he still has the perspective of the old response and knows that the old response is still available. Culture operates most effectively in the area of standard response to old situations.

New situations bring forth difficulties. If the event is in fact too different, no behavior may result because the individual does not know what to do; he has no appropriate nomeme to guide him. Often the person tries to apply an old response, a response that is inappropriate to the problem. Probably the most common action is to apply a response on the basis of analogical features. That is, he perceives the problem, relates it as closely as possible to similar problems he is familiar with and uses the nomemes appropriate to the familiar problem.

Man's powerful memory makes it possible for behavioral acts to originate internally without the immediate external presence of a stimulus. By recall a person may activate his brain and set behavior in motion without visible external origins. Such behavior arising from internal or memory sources often creates confusion because other individuals cannot perceive its beginnings. The person himself may be unaware of the origins of his activity. Furthermore, because every individual has recorded a great number of sensory impressions his memory can provide vastly more stimulation to behavior at any one time than he might receive from the immediate external world. Simultaneously there may be an arousal of the emotional response associated with the original stimulus. Responses may overlap or conflict with each other producing uncertainty, doubt, and anxiety. The individual may recall the incident over and over again and transfer and rearrange segments since they only exist in the fluid structure of his mind.

Culture is dependent upon standard cognitive processes found in many animal forms. The differences
lie in the fact that humans have greater capacity to
store and recall senory impressions than other animals,
and have language and shared experience. Furthermore,
humans can not only recall sensory impressions, they
can also recall their recall of sensory impressions. It
is this second level abstraction that enables the human
to observe himself and his own cognitive existence.
The experiential variables affecting acquired response
provide the varied behavioral patterns found in different
individuals. These individual behavior patterns develop
because no two individuals have the same identical
experiences and hence each accumulates a different
set of specific nomemes to guide activity. Man is a
biological constant but his individual behavior nevertheless varies radically according to his culture and
his personal experiences.

CHAPTER SEVEN

THE ROOTS OF CULTURE

The man we see today walking, talking, fighting, and loving, can hardly be imagined differently. His arms, his hands, his legs all function to perform the tasks of life. He conjures up the immense emotions of hate, love, and anger. He constructs language and writes books. But in reality he is but a moment of time in the process of an evolving being who has been in the making for millions of years. This being is not the product of a simple linear development or a direct biological evolution but is the result of a constant interplay between what he was, what he learns, and what he has to be. From far back in history man has been a dual creature operating both in the biological and the cultural realms. His increasing volume of accumulated and transmittable instructions existed in an organic and real world. It was exposed to the same pressures, to the same kinds of selective processes as are all other changes and adaptive developments. Some nomemes increased the life expectancy of individuals and their groups. They survived, became part of the cultural pool. Others did not and faded out of existence.

Culture did not begin from the conscious manipulations of any particular man, from his insight or foresight. It grew out of the undirected process of selective adaptation, from the continuous biological and environmental pressures occurring on every side. There was no single point in time, no single place where man suddenly appeared and began using culture. Culture and man emerged simultaneously, and became one.

From the very beginning of man as a cultural being, however, he had some capacity to accumulate experience to create nomemes in such a way as to affect his future behavior. This capacity was minimal in the beginning, gradually increasing over time as the brain grew in response to behavioral demands.

For hundreds and even thousands of generations, man constructed, developed and abstracted principles and plans which were useful in his battle to survive. These nomemes have been added to, modified, reinterpreted, and abandoned countless times during the course of history. Not all disappeared for many early nomemes remain with us in the form of superstitions, myths, folktales, etiquette, and other residuals.

Each cultural invention had a potential for affecting the genetic pool. Every biological response made by the species presented the possibility of further cultural creations. The growth of the brain was related to the growth of intelligence which was related to man's increasing reliance upon culture. With the expansion of intelligence there was a corresponding loss of dependence upon innate predispositions. The increased brain size and complexity led to an accompanying growth of knowledge. Longer and longer periods of time were necessary for the acquisition of this knowledge. Infancy, childhood, and adolescence gradually became stretched out until today they are twice as long as found in the nearest primate. Selective factors were at work also in terms of individual educatability, control of emotions, and cooperative ability.

Culture is firmly founded in the physical characteristics of man and in his biological history. These characteristics did not always exist. Most of this biological story will never be known and can only be speculated about. But pivotal points exist in the development of these morphological features. They occurred so far back in time that there are only the barest hints about their origins. Nevertheless looking at the vast time-line over which these changes took place, they can be arranged in some kind of order. Obviously such conjectures are merely efforts to understand an immense complexity. The order of biological development appears to have been changes in eye structure, the hands, the shoulder girdle, a shift to upright posture, and the loss of body hair.

Cultural development and the related biological changes exist in a reciprocal relationship. Nevertheless the logical sequence that must have occurred can be deduced. Despite the fact that culture has no precise beginning date, it is possible to divide the evolution of culture into some general stages. The first stage finds the early manforms acting in largely animal and genetically controlled ways. They were probably already using nomemes emphasizing group life and a socio-spatial organization much like the modern Kenya baboon. These nomemes, simple as they were, dramatically increased the life expectancy of individual members. An isolated baboon has little chance of survival if he does not belong to a troop, and early men undoubtedly experienced much the same kind of advantage from troop life. Nomemes for the employment of elementary signalling devices were already being used, just as dogs bark or chimpanzees chatter. All existing primates have their signalling systems which not only are effective because of group life, but at the same time act to preserve that very groupness. This stage then is marked by ground living individuals who were using elementary signalling systems, walking upright, using a home base, and who were relatively hairless.

The next stage is marked by the development of nomemes for the use of naturally occurring tools of wood, bone, or stone. Tool use was of two types. Initially tools were relatively unmodified and were used only sporadically and temporarily. Modern chimpanzees provide insight into tool use at this stage, often picking up branches, sticks, or stones at a time of crisis. They can be seen vigorously shaking branches on trees or bouncing on limbs near predators. They obviously know that the unnatural movement of a tree or a branch is frightening to other animals. Occasionally they accidentally break off the branches in their exuberance and simply wave the broken branches or beat them on the ground. When branches are not available, or they are on the ground, they seize dead limbs for the same purpose. Their aim at throwing or beating is often very haphazard and inaccurate and they probably are not so intent upon hitting an intruder, for example, as simply making a lot of movement and noise. But as man evolved he discovered that hitting an attacker was also effective.

Stage three arose when complex nomemes were developed for the conscious shaping and retention of tools. No composite tools yet existed, merely shaped wooden clubs and stone objects like balls or sharp flakes. It is this point that many scholars believe to be the really significant threshold of culture. By this time the human brain had developed a special capacity to make and use nomemes, to associate across receptors, to use speech, to symbolize and abstract at a high level.

The period during which man used only simple and crude tools is an exceedingly long portion of human existence. If one were to imagine that the last million years was represented by a thousand-page book with each page covering one thousand years then it would be necessary to devote five hundred pages to stage three alone. In reality this period may have been several times as long. At the very end of this period or perhaps even later, the use of fire, clothing, and shelters began and developed. The use of these tools reflected several things; the continued growth and accumulation of effective nomemes, an expansion in basic intellectual ability, and an increased ability to observe and memorize. The critical factor was the ability to differentiate between various kinds of physical objects and to see in their natural appearance a potential utility. The need to recognize various natural materials in terms of different kinds of characteristics led to a greater awareness and discriminating ability in other areas including self-awareness. Most animals are content to merely distinguish food objects from non-food objects and harmful from non-harmful things but man goes far beyond that.

Man's ability to create a mental image not only in the presence of an object but also when the object was no longer present had greatly increased. This was a part of the ability to visualize the utility of a stone or piece of wood and led to true symbolization, to the substitution of an abstract symbol in place of the concrete reality. It was this unique ability of man that lies at the base of true cultural development.

Despite many similarities, the human mind does differ from the mind of other animals in a very significant way. This difference is closely associated with the interrelated evolution of the hand, the brain, and speech. The hand enables objects to be grasped and brought closer to the eyes for visual inspection. Primates are more proficient hand users than other animals and many of them can grasp and manipulate objects in a simple way. Primates generally use either hand indiscriminately but when in the past the prehuman primates began using sticks and stones for tools they started a new evolutionary direction. This came about because many simple tools are better handled with one hand at a time, and hand preference develops. It was not important which hand was originally used. The important thing was that it was only one hand. Because of the differential use of the hands in managing tools, and the fact that each hand is tied more closely to the cerebral area of one hemisphere of the brain than it is to the other, there is a potential for affecting the development and evolution of each hemisphere in different ways.

The early tool using activities of mankind were extremely simple and consisted of merely picking up stones, carrying them, throwing, pounding, clubbing, and hitting. Nevertheless even these simple activities began to have a profound effect upon the neural organization and development of the brain. The right hand gradually became preferred over the left and as a result the left hemisphere of the brain was the most affected. In a sense, it became specialized to manage the right hand, while the right hemisphere continued to function as it had. The split in functions between the two halves of the brain made possible activities previously unimaginable.

Animals with nondifferentiated hemispheres produce behavior, but none of them have the abilities made possible by the special quality of the left hemisphere of the human brain. Among those behaviors now more realizable was the greater ability to symbolize. While the unraveling of causal relationships is complex and tenuous, the man made tool appears to have been the critical factor. This comes about because a tool is a future directed symbol, that is, the construction of a tool and its subsequent use requires a comprehension of objects and events in the future. One recognizes in a sharp stone the potential for skinning a slain animal, or in a round stone, a weapon that can be thrown. The sharp stone becomes a symbol for the future act of cutting. Seeing a sharp stone can stimulate the image of cutting something; a dead animal can stimulate the image of a sharp stone.

At this stage the image symbols are private, existing only in the mind of the individual. Sight is its own symbol and is largely personal. Sound on the other hand had been used for ages to convey the affective states of fear, anger, and danger in a plural personal way. The fact that tools were symbols connected with the right hand led to a concentration of symbolizing ability in the left hemisphere. When vocal symbols were substituted for the visual concept the vocal symbol was also managed in the left hemisphere.

There are few means for revealing the development of the mind of early man. But there are some fragmentary hints. The shape, standardization, and function of tools provides the major source of information. Drawings, paintings, etchings and sculptures found on cave walls, antlers, and stone slabs also provide clues. Scratches, incised lines, chevrons and wavy marks indicate something about the mental processes of these early humans. They are clear indications that these creatures were purposefully making figures on selected materials, that they could control the lines they made and, therefore, could control their hand-eye coordination activities. They often kept their drawings and periodically added other marks to them which indicates they knew what the previous marks meant and could meaningfully interpret them, add to them and expect other people to understand them. Another valuable clue lies in the shape of lithic tools themselves. While the number of tool types was very restricted during the early stages of tool making it could be expected that there would be great differences between tools in different regions in terms of size, shape, and materials utilized. Yet over vast stretches of the sparsely populated world, there is a remarkable standardization of handaxes and other stone implements. Most are made from moderately hard crystalline rock that fractures into sharp-edged flakes. The basic shape of the handaxe was very similar all over its distribution, tapering in a tear drop shape from a broad rounded end to a sharp point with two cutting edges. Because of the different specific stone used to make these tools it is clear they were not all manufactured in one place and disseminated by trade. Nor is there any evidence that bands of skilled artisans wandered from group to group making and trading tools for food and shelter as in a later day.

A certain amount of standardization can be expected because of the necessity for the tool to conform to the human hand, and to be related to its intended use. Yet there were alternative shapes that tools could have taken and still been useful. There must be other explanations for this early and very widespread standardization, for while a paleolithic stone axe may appear simple, its manufacture in actuality requires considerable knowledge and skill. One cannot just go out and pick up any odd piece of rock and fashion a handaxe. It is apparent, therefore, that at a very early time, all the nomemes and instructions for making handaxes had been developed, that man was capable of communicating these nomemes, and that other men could comprehend them. In other words there existed an idealized cognitive image, model or prototype of a completed axe and all the steps necessary to produce it. Apparently, at the beginning of human history only a single set of nomemes had been developed, and this set spread far and wide, over Africa, Europe, and parts of Asia.

When the immensity of the meaning of this standardization is realized, it provides a whole new stream of insights about the development of cultural history and the nature of culture. The key here is the fact that with any complex object, merely observing the finished product is insufficient experience for duplicating it. No one can manufacture a handaxe without a great deal of direct teaching exposure and controlled learning. First one must recognize that the axe is of stone, and not just any stone, but a particular kind of stone. Shaping the stone after it has been selected requires understanding the nature of the material and the nature of the actions that must be used. Without careful observation of the actual process and learning the nomemes of percussion-flaking, the resultant tool would probably not duplicate the prototype and its usefulness would be doubtful. Somehow the early makers of stone tools developed sets of operating nomemes regarding the finding, selecting, and shaping of raw stone and other materials into finished products. And even more astonishing than the ability to conceptualize the necessary tasks in order of their priority was the ability to teach others the sets of nomemes, spreading a concept of tool manufacturing over thousands of miles and hundreds of generations.

It has long been thought that the development of true symbolic language communication was a slow evolutionary process, and it may well have been so. But there is a seminal conjunction between the close of the middle Paleolithic period and the rise of modern man about 35,000 years ago, in terms of a sudden increase and quality of material culture. It is possible that a pivotal point occurred here in terms of communication ability which led then to a spectacular expansion of culture. This break-through might well be correlated with a significant change in the brain or the vocal apparatus.

Culture originated, then, as part of the evolutionary process which extended genetic and instinctual tools enabling early man to take greater advantage of his learning ability. This advantage consisted in part in the capability to accumulate and consolidate the experiences of a number of individuals and to shape subsequent behavior through the lessons learned from life. A second level of existence of a cultural world resulted, where behavior was derived, not from direct experience, but from cultural traditions. This includes making tools with other tools, preparing for marriage before one is married, experiencing a book someone else has written.

During the hundreds of thousands of years of prehistoric time, both the human being as a biological entity and as a cultural being took the direction and thrust that has shaped and governed man and society to this day. The great tides were established in those distant ages. Man must continue to contend with those cultural-behavioral structures created at the dawn of history. The structure of the brain, his hand-eye coordination, his physiological response to stress, his imagination, and problem solving all began long ago. He became a maker and user of tools and a maker and user of tools he continues to be. It is improbable that the basic concerns and pursuits of humanity are to be soon abandoned. There will be further modifications, more sophisticated machinery, new sources of energy made captive, more subtle distinctions in defining the roles of the sexes. But the changes as they come will not be arbitrary or capricious; they will come in response to experiential necessities, and the making will be molded by existing cultural plans. The hope for wisdom will become brighter as men come to better understand the human cultural apparatus.

CHAPTER EIGHT

CULTURE, SOCIETY AND HUMAN LIFE

For culture to be effective or to exist at all, there must be human groups. For groups to be effective there must be culture. Therefore it is no surprise to find that humans everywhere exist in groups. But groups do not either form themselves or function automatically. They all face the same fundamental problems, getting people together, keeping them together, and getting them to function effectively together.

Like other aspects of behavior, the structure and activities of groups are dependent upon the nomemes the group develops. Like the interaction between an athletic team and the rules of the game, groups are related to culture. Each is indispensible to the other and while the ultimate goal is the successful functioning of individual members of the group, this is best achieved when the group and the culture are in unison.

Although groups come in many sizes and compositions, in general they can be differentiated into two broad classes, the categorical groups and the interaction groups. These two types of groupings are very different but often confused. When one speaks of categorical groups, one means only that some people can be thought of as alike, that they have some common behavioral or other characteristic that links them to other people who have similar characteristics. A categorical group may be comprised of alcoholics, red headed people, children of astronauts, ex-convicts, widows, or retired executives. They belong to a category, but the significant factor is that they do not necessarily interact or have any contact with each other. They exist as a group because cognitively and verbally it is useful, not because they perform any group function.

Interaction groups, on the other hand, exist because the members have some form of relatively continuous interpersonal contact and interdependence. They may consist of members of an office staff, an athletic team, a family, or a tribe. Some kind of interaction network includes all members, and in some degree, all members subscribe to a shared set of behavioral nomemes.

Interaction groups themselves can be based either in principles of solidarity or of function. Solidarity groups are primarily concerned with the well being of the members, of taking care of the social and life needs of the individuals who make up the group. Functional groups, on the other hand, are more concerned with accomplishing some objective, of successfully completing some task. In solidarity groups the individual is the end, in the functional group, the individual is primarily a means to an end.

The principles governing the founding of these two types of groups are radically different. The good of the society comes first in the solidarity group. Consequently, all the nomemes that follow from this principle will be consistent with its purpose. For example, another premise that might derive immediately from the first premise states; behavior that is for the good of society will also be good for the individual.

Functional or task oriented groups are based on the concept that completing the task comes before the welfare of any individual. In this system people exist merely to perform certain functions and the directors of the task are not concerned with the individual as a person except insofar as he is related to the success of the operation. Thus the nomemes employed emphasize primarily those behaviors necessary to perform the task.

The history of the evolution of social systems seems to indicate two things: societies have increasingly moved toward the functional model, especially in modern commercial and industrial nations; secondly, the larger the society becomes the more task oriented and impersonal relationships between people become. Because functional groups focus more on task goals and less on meeting the needs of the individual members, commitment and loyalty of the members is often much less than it is in solidarity groups. This often leads to a feeling of not knowing where he belongs on the part of the individual.

The nomemes that lie at the base of social structure and which regulate interaction among group members have two origins and these result in two different kinds of societies. The most common source, and one which has prevailed in most small scale and non-industrial societies, is the members who compose the group. Everyone has an opportunity to originate behavior which is then accepted or rejected on the basis of perceived utility and group evaluation.

In the other system, nomemes originate from a central source, either a particular individual or a role position and are disseminated throughout the group in the form of orders or rules. In this type of system the society itself may be structured as a series of vertically organized power positions. Origination and response to nomemes are essentially a one way process, while in the other system it is a two way process. The power systems tend to have more disciplinary problems and often must use force to suppress behavior inconsistent with the intent of the control group. Egalitarian societies on the other hand, by their very nature, are more democratic and receptive to individual expression. In power societies discipline and enforcement are imposed from above, usually through a system of hierarchial ordered authority positions which are related to certain duties and rewards. But in democratically organized societies adherence to standards of acceptable behavior is a result of cultural enculturation and are self-imposed although mediated by public opinion.

Within the structure of a society the prevailing thrust of behavior that people take relative to other people can be thought of as having two potentials. On the one hand, it can be cooperative and aimed at being helpful to others; or it can be competitive and designed to use and take advantage of others. Societies that are predominately competitive, such as modern America, tend to make individuals feel that they are different and unique and that they occupy an inferior or superior relationship to others. On the other hand, an egalitarian society, such as the Hopi strives to make everyone feel more or less equal and to suppress behavior aimed at establishing a superior-inferior status relationship.

Societies are primarily interaction groups although they also contain within their parameters all categorical groups. There are many different reasons for the existence of specific societies but the general reasons are the same. Even before mankind emerged it was discovered that several individuals working together were more successful in repelling a predator or hunting the evening meal than a single individual acting alone. While random aggregation and grouping does exist, societies are formed of people who share reasons and means for relatively continuous interaction and are not the result of chance or fortuitous gatherings There must be a purpose for interaction groups to exist and cohesive means for binding members together.

The primary reason people gathered together to form the first rudimentary societies was for the protection that the presence of large, powerful, or wise individuals gave to the weak and the helpless. Weak individuals, including pregnant females, females with infants, and the young and juvenile, stayed near large and powerful males because they had learned that they were safer there. The males themselves did not form or lead these groups but merely continued their normal routines moving where they wished to, eating when they wanted, and seeking shelter when they were ready. To have the protection of the powerful males the weaker individuals followed them about, staying as close as possible without actually interfering with them. Their presence nearby made two other types of behavior available: group activity and cooperation for reproductive purposes. The need for sexual interaction is a powerful force acting on each human but it is not as critical to the formation of society as the presence of security and protection. Sexual activity is occasional, intermittent and temporary, but protection is a constant need. Strong and capable individuals everywhere form a focus about which the weaker gather, and undoubtedly the first social nomemes were related to this principle.

Among humans the first initial impetus to groupness has been vastly extended by the creation of a net of nomemes to increase cooperative behavior in other critical areas of common activity. These areas of common activity included the production and care of offspring, the development of a communication system and the procuring of food. Nomemes had to be developed to manage the mating relationship and to establish responsibility for providing for children. The mother-father and husband-wife relationship had to be clarified and regularized because of the necessity for assigning responsibility to certain individuals for others. Thus a mother was seen as having greater responsibility for her child than other children, a man who was habitually with a woman had responsibility for her during her pregnancy and eventually for her infant; and children had responsibility for their elderly parents. People who lived together had greater responsibility for each other than for others, and those who were perceived as relatives, had greater responsibility for each other than for nonrelatives.

Primarily, then, society is another expression of man's need for order and for controlling the future. It is an effort to organize people in such a way that their behavior has some predictability and regularity. Order-liness in society is created through cultural nomemes and structural organization. Social organization not only functions to further human cooperation but in addition strengthens and regulates the very elements that brought people together initially.

Social nomemes are generated out of the recurrent and collective activities of group members   from the routines and emergencies of everyday life. As members interact with each other, as they hunt or farm, build houses or boats, they develop standard nomemes of behavior, common beliefs and principles. From the shared aspects of their life they shape a culture. These behavioral nomemes are closely related to the particular life situation facing the group: to the necessity of finding food in the Arctic cold, to the difficulty of locating water in deserts, the danger from predators in jungles, and to the events in the group's history. Plans and nomemes reinforce the social order and in turn are supported by that order. The result is a unity, stability and efficiency far beyond the herd aspect of gregariousness.

The social structure itself, the relationships of various components, the associations and institutions, like the rooms of a house, are related to each other through size, position, and activities. They each must relate and function relative to all other segments. They are not autonomous, separate, and independent. Behind the complexities of social structure lie nomemes and principles just like those that shape all other aspects of human behavior. Without such nomemes the capacity to form social groups of any kind would be extremely limited.

Group activities, activities dependent upon numbers of individuals rather than single individuals, are the critical factor in society. The game of tennis requires two players, basketball ten. Neither game can be played without sufficient members. Society operates in a similar but far more complex manner. The games societal groups play require multiple numbers of players and are impossible without a minimum number, but difficult when too many try to play.

The ultimate premise then upon which groupness and society is based, is personal security. Every individual recognizes his openness to physical attack, his vulnerability to harm, the threats upon his life from other persons and creatures. He seeks as his primary task the establishment of a relationship of trust and reliability with other individuals which will provide him some security. This relationship must be one he can depend upon to assist him in time of danger, and which will help him meet the needs of existence. Society begins with this individual, this solitary person looking out upon a vast world with its potential hostility and danger.

As the individual strives to build a circle of people around him upon whom he can rely and trust he most often turns to his parents, his grandparents, his siblings, and his family group. These people themselves have gone through the same process of identifying and creating a reliability group, a process that began with the procreative act and the requirements of rearing and protecting the young. While the initial relationship is between father and mother, this contact is often so momentary and tenuous that the really binding force in the creation of a family group is the dependence of the helpless infant upon the mother. The infant's first social nomeme then is concerned with establishing strong reliable bonds with those who will care for him. He does this by the curiosity that his presence arouses in others, by his infantile cuteness, by smiling and otherwise wooing those around him who could destroy him in seconds.

Beyond the immediate family cluster, he soon discovers there lies a ring of relatives who are not directly related, but are linked to him only through another person, and which includes uncles, aunts, and grandparents. Beyond those relatives are still others related through two intermediate persons such as cousins and great-grandparents. These rings of relatives and kin fade away into neighbors, friends, acquaintances, and finally to strangers and enemies. Thus each individual comes to exist in a vast surrounding envelope of people graded according to their relationship and reliability. Relatives are often bound together in units beyond the family, into clans and lineages, and eventually into communities, villages, and even tribal and national unions.

Families are interaction groups and basically solidarity groups as well. The functions they perform are for the benefit of family members and generally speaking not for the purpose of reaching some impersonal goal. Families tend to be hierarchially ordered with the power lying with the head of the family. This is a natural outcome of age, sex, and generational differences. Between families and between members of equal age and sex egalitarian principles may supersede power principles, however.

It is easy to idealize the security found in family relationships, yet they have far greater reliability on the whole than chance or accidental relationships. In a world full of life-threatening situations, any advantage created by an association of persons will have survival value, and the more binding factors there are holding the group together, the more effective it will be.

But knowing who one's relatives are, and what degree of relationship they have is not simple. Because of the great number of relatives one has and the infrequency which one may see all of them, it is necessary that some system be devised that will enable one to identify other kin-related persons and to know how to treat and be treated by them. This is accomplished by reducing the number of individuals to a workable size by grouping them into categories. So while a person might not be able to remember each relative individually, it is possible through this system for him to remember to which category they belong and thus know how to behave toward them.

The first great division of relatives one recognizes are either the mother's side of the family or the father's side. The second great division is that of people related by birth and those related by marriage. Each of these divisions have their separate nomemes that establish the kind of relationships that will prevail between people of the different groups.

Marriage raises some critical problems for the

individual and the group; for it joins to one's family of birth another group of families. Choosing a marriage partner presents a dilemma for the family and the nomemes of marriage reflect this. The problem is whether one should consolidate the strengths of the family by ingroup marriage and increase the intensity of the reliability structure, or should one marry outside the family to enlarge the size of the reliability group through incorporating another family. Whether one marries endogamously or exogamously depends upon the kind of danger present, the weaknesses and strengths of the two family groups, and perhaps the distance separating them. Few families are willing to let their sons or daughters marry into distant groups where they will not be able to exercise some protection for them.

While kinship nomemes provide the fundamental force controlling group organization in simple societies, other group producing forces are at work. These include the natural setting of landscape and environment, population characteristics, biological attributes, materials and technology as well as the effect of historic events. Individuals who share a region have greater opportunity to influence each others' thoughts and actions. Proximity and common environment channel local groups to develop nomemes for cooperating and sharing many aspects of life. People become deeply involved with the topography, the environmental resources, and limitations of their territory. They come to know where the game animals live, where certain plants grow, where good farming land is found, and where the best trees occur. The amount of land which can be cognitively exploited by an individual or group is limited. The number of people which an area will support is also limited. The land that can support a group, which can be cognitively exploited and which is physically occupied and defended constitutes the group's territory. This region is thought of as belonging to the group, but just as importantly, the members of the group think of themselves as belonging to the land. It is theirs. It is vital to their existence, a

fact of which they are constantly aware. It is critical
because of their exploitative knowledge. Their nomemes
are intimately connected with that particular piece of
land. Moved elsewhere, the nomemes that a man
utilizes to hunt may no longer apply to the animals of
the new region; the nomemes his wife uses do not
enable her to tell the edible plants from the non-edible
or how to prepare them. In short the land is their life
and a change which is too radical makes it difficult to
apply the cultural strategies upon which they are
dependent, and will lead to their suffering and even
extinction.

As one proceeds outward from the family core, the
relationships and degree of reliability become more and
more tenuous and vague until a point is reached where
nomemes of another kind must be developed. This
usually occurs on the fringe of the group's territory,
where other locality groups are encountered. These
groups normally cannot be ignored and they are significant since they establish the boundaries of the group
The new relationship cannot depend upon kinship ties
for its effectiveness but must create a political form
of organization and behavior. Political activity tends
to emerge at the point where family and kinship power
begins to lose its effectiveness. Political activity
can take many shapes including war, marriage, trade
or confederation. But whatever interactions are to
occur, regular procedures for dealing with the problem
of neighboring locality groups must be developed.

Locality groups have names taken from geographic
features, peculiar appearance, or great deeds. They
may be called Bitter Water people, Many Goats, or
Mountaineers. Often they adopt a name taken from an
animal or plant found in their territory such as wallaby
kangaroo or emu. The members in a sense have a
common surname, Lion, Bear, or Wolf. They may also
be in fact descendants of an old man named Wallaby or
Lion, and they think of this old man as an ancestral
god and supernatural procreator. They refrain from
killing the totem animal because there is a nomeme
prohibiting the killing of a relative. Within their

territory, the animal is sacred and secure.

Surrounding them on all sides are other groups with their territories, their totems, and their sacred places. In those localities other totem animals are sheltered and protected. Thus in a large region there will be a number of contiguous tribal territories, each offering protection for a particular totem animal. Since groups rarely cross territorial boundaries, what really exists is a series of animal refuges wherein critical species are protected to serve as a breeding population for the surrounding areas where they are readily hunted.

Another important factor that must be accounted for in group formation is the fact that people come in two sexes and in many ages. Recognized or not, sex-age groups occur in every society. Usually there are explicit nomemes of speech, dress, mannerisms, and expectations that take them into account. Status and roles--the nomemes of social position and behavior-- are based on age and sex. They are related to the fundamental imperatives of pregnancy and bearing children, and the conditions of the life cycle. Neither age nor sex totally determines social behavior and particular individuals may ignore them, but society as a whole cannot.

An overriding consideration in all functioning soc- ieties is the fact that they share language. It is obvious but often forgotten that for languages to be effective, groups of speakers are necessary. Language implies groupness. Speech is directed at others in the expectation that they will hear and understand. To be understood requires finding someone who speaks your language. Language forms groups and ties people together just as do other cultural activities. Behavior, to be meaningful, requires a common understanding of the shared plans. Shared nomemes create groups, and language, therefore, is one of the most powerful social cohesives.

Instructions and nomemes are apt to become diluted and variant, at the edges of any society. In the marginal regions where contact exists with other com- munities, a tribal culture may be subject to influence from the adjacent group. It is at this point that principles of ethnocentrism, or belief in the superiority of one's own group, arises. These beliefs preserve and enhance the local group's culture, and the individual's personal identity. Ethnocentrism is a vital component in the maintenance of groupness, but at the same time tends to inhibit cross-group understanding.

Interest groups are composed of people who are tied together by a concern about some special facet of life. Interest groups may or may not interact. Stamp club members, gamblers, baseball fans, art lovers, are drawn together to show and develop their common interest. Common interest may also exist in other groups. Family members are generally tied to each other by shared interests, and age group concerns are also efficient social binders.

Common tasks are cohesive factors that hold groups together. Task groups are an important aspect of every societies' existence. They may be long term, such as a standing army or a ship's crew, or a short term appointed committee. Bureaucratic and business organized groups are task oriented. Task groups have people who direct and people who execute the directions. They have a hierarchical order in that they are organized by an increasing complexity of skills and duties. This order arises because tasks are often sequential and the sequence must be understood and operationalized in order for the task to be completed. The classification of the major task, the division into sub-tasks, and the sequencing of these, are merely a formalizing of the nomemes that exist throughout any society. The task itself then serves to tie the members of the group together.

Sub-Cultures

Other kinds of groups are often found in large societies. Their presences as small minorities within the larger groups are sometimes perplexing. Sub-group members share many culture features among themselves, but as a group they differ from the major community in perceivable behavior or appearance. They originate in two different ways, and can be thought of either as derivative or parallel. Derivative sub-cultures are split off from the parent society and eventually do not share all the dominant cultural themes. Parallel sub-cultures exist within, or adjacent to, the major culture. Their origins and development are separate, however. American Indians, Jews, Mexican-Americans all live in parallel sub-cultures to the national culture in America. They are not derived from the primary culture, but are separate and move through history in a parallel relationship. They are part of the history of the majority society but not of it.

These distinctions are ideal. In reality there is much overlap, much direct and indirect influence back and forth. Under these circumstances individuals often become confused by not knowing to which culture they belong. Traditional parents do not understand their children and children do not understand their parents. Teachers and officials of the majority society may not understand either the parents nor the children. Sub-cultures develop from physical and social isolation, differences in ethnic origins, in languages, or situational factors of wealth or poverty. Vocational and occupational specializations may separate people, create sub-groups, which may result in antagonism, hatreds, and schisms.

It has been popular recently in America to speak of another type of sub-society, that of adolescence. It is called a counter culture since it is so often an expression of opposition to the dominant society. But is it a real culture? Does it have its own nomemes passed from generation to generation and does it arise from the interaction of group members? Only in part. It encompasses only a few of the life tasks and, in this sense, is only a partial culture. It is involved primarily with social behavior, vocabulary, clothes, cars, and recreation. It is primarily an arena for establishing personal identity and lacks the wholeness of general culture. It is very little concerned with the

major business of life, with providing shelter, sub-
sistence, and defending itself against external forces.
It is a phase, a pseudo culture, an expression of the
growth pattern. It arises out of the uncertainty of the
role of youth in modern life.

It has been common in America to think that young
people naturally experience both psychological trauma
and tendencies toward non-conformity as they strive
for adulthood. But both of these expressions are cultural and learned. They are not universal outgrowths
of the biology of adolescence. Despite the outward
show of resistance to the national culture through its
aberrant behavior and its counter elements, teenage
behavior displays many characteristics of culture as a
system of behavior. Its dominant trait is its uni-
formity, its conformity to youth ideals. It is a
collateral culture rather than a generation one, that
is, a peer culture. The peer group has a powerful
attraction and a special salvation. To the members it
provides shelter and strength and freedom of behavior.
The young feel they can trust their age mates more than
others. Their comrades do not have the strength,
experience, or power to dominate and take advantage
of them the same way adults can. The youth can trust
his age mates more because, in general, they are
experiencing the same problems he is. He can better
share experiences with others who understand them.

Yet the peer group can be one of the most tyrannical
of forces bearing on the youth. Because the desire to
be accepted by peer mates is so strong, the peer group
can take advantage of this to force young people into
harmful behavior. Nomemes are rigidly observed
regarding what to do, how to do it, what to wear, what
to say, and where to be. An adolescent who does not
know the vocabulary of this culture is ostracized as
strange or deviant. He must live alone, unable to
participate and share his life experiences.

The reason for youth culture seems clear enough. In
America the adolescent and child are excluded from
real participation in the life of the society because
the society is largely a task or functional group and

youth has no real part to play. The young are often treated as fixtures or ornaments for their parents' benefit, and are seldom permitted to do anything real and meaningful. The lack of correspondence between what they are told and what they see engenders disillusionment and lack of respect for adults. In fact, it is difficult to fit young people today meaningfully into mainstream activity. There are child work laws, compulsory schooling, and insurance clauses that restrict real participation in industry and commerce. Meanwhile children are told fairy tales about adult life. They are lectured on honesty and fairness and see cheating and dishonesty all around them. They are sermoned on the virtues of Christianity but see too many Sunday practitioners. They are told about democracy but read about racial and religious prejudices, bigotry, denial of voting rights, political payoffs, and crime in daily floods. They are excluded from real participation in the national life, yet are pawns for adults. They are inducted into the military system or school system without voice and without recourse. They are slaves of a different order, but still slaves. They lack meaningful guidance and activities; they experience only surveillance and supervision. Barred from the major activities of the national society they are at the same time thrown together. They strive to develop a meaningful behavioral framework within the interstices of the dominant culture. Their culture becomes a closed system with its own nomemes, signals, and membership. The flouting of national cultural nomemes becomes a theme that grew out of the involuntary rejection by the majority society.

This youth culture is a powerful force. It recruits through the knowledge that in American society, the adolescent is facing new kinds of anxiety producing problems which he is not given the means to resolve. Since all culture acts as a security base in this sense, providing an aspect of certainty and reliability to the individual, the adolescent seeking some cultural acceptance finds it only among other rejected adolescents. He is willing to sacrifice his own individuality, his parents, his family, or his adult future to achieve some cultural foundations during this period of perceived need. He may, in reality, care nothing for smoking, drugs, alcohol, or racing cars, but he must pretend to do so in order to have a sense of belonging to a cultural group. The need for culture is the most powerful force acting upon any individual.

The dissatisfactions that adolescent culture reflects demonstrate that every society must provide means for all its membership to participate. No one can be left out. Providing meaningful positions for everyone in the group is one of the most urgent and difficult tasks of any society. Everyone must be fitted into the cultural operation. People who are left out, and this includes youth, and who consequently fail to benefit by the existing cultural order, are disgruntled and unhappy. They provide a source of potential danger to the equilibrium of the system.

When society does not provide means for satisfying either the basic biological or social needs of an individual, the individual will either move to a society that does satisfy his needs or he will attempt to alter the present society so that his needs are met. Social commitment and cohesion are dependent upon how well the society satisfies the basic and social needs of its members. The degree of conformity a society can require of an individual and the amount of conformity the individual will tolerate are related to the degree which the society satisfies the needs of the individual.

In a society which is numerically increasing, the difficulty of providing cultural positions for the rising generation presents a massive problem. It is a problem for many reasons, but primarily because the better social and economic positions are already occupied by entrenched older members, a situation of which the incoming generation is well aware. This forces the majority of young people to start at the bottom of the social ladder and work upward through the ranks. This situation is galling because it implies that age and first rights are more important than ability, worth, and need. Furthermore, there is an assumption that the incoming generation values the cultural positions which have been established for it. But in the modern, rapidly changing world, members of the incoming generation do not necessarily desire to be heirs to a cultural structure with its allotted slots constructed by a preceding generation. They wish to construct their own slots on their own terms. In fact, in many instances this is the only possibility since all existing slots are already occupied.

In well-established and relatively stable cultural organizations, the movement of an individual through a series of cultural positions during his lifetime is clear, predictable, and provides a great deal of security and order to a person's existence. In modern American society, the flux of the situation makes it impossible for the cultural pattern to be grasped by the incoming generation. The national culture is so abstract as to be incomprehensible. Groups function in unseen patterns. To many it appears to be a fragmented society. There are too many governmental levels, too many conflicting laws, too much mobility and change to understand. Too much of one's energies are spent simply trying to grasp the patterns of life with little time left for living.

Consequently, since they cannot see the order, the incoming generation rejects, and rightly so, the uncertainty of that culture and strives to construct a culture where their position is understandable. It is a fundamental function of culture to make clear and understandable the life path of the individual.

The Culture of Poverty Concept

The use of the culture of poverty concept is another example of a phrase with many implications in current use. This phrase implies that poor people, relatively speaking, share a body of cultural characteristics and constitute a sub-culture. But as many societies have poor people, there are many circumstances under which the culture of poverty occurs. If the subgroup of poverty is a deviant form of the larger body then it will show many characteristics of that body. Therefore, the cultural characteristics of each group of poor includes features which distinguish it from the main cultural body and these features would be different for each poverty group because the larger social body of which they are a part is unique from all others.

What occurs, however, is that poor people everywhere in all societies share some common characteristics as a result of being poor. They share some situational and statistical similarities which mistakenly have been called cultural. There exists also a strong implication that poverty brings about poverty as a result of some causal effect of the culture of poverty. This may be partially true, but in reality what occurs is that poverty everywhere has certain conditions which tend to produce a particular behavioral response. This is usually different and distinguishable from the majority culture. Poor people are not successful in competing with the members of the majority culture. What is not realized is that the culture of poverty is not merely a crude and incomplete form of the majority culture, but everywhere is an adaptive technique when other cultural directions are forbidden or unavailable. In this case, the culture of poverty does not refer to a cultural tradition produced by an interacting group of people having both a locality and a history, but to a common response to a situation in which many avenues of cultural behavior participated in by the majority are blocked. If similar behavioral nomemes have developed among widely dispersed people in many different societies, it is a case of parallelism rather than dissemination.

It is true, however, that in particular areas, the poor do appear to have a behavior related to poverty which is transmitted from generation to generation. These cultural features do often appear to discourage the poor moving out of the poverty cycle. Cultural nomemes expressed as attitudes toward work, money, children, and learning are passed on from parents to children and when these fail to correspond to the beliefs held by the dominant powers in the society, the poor cannot achieve the kind of success that would lift them out of their poverty status. These cultural traits then do contribute to keeping the poor poor.

More importantly, the poor in America represent a class conflict. In a nation so immense, it is useless to speak of a single culture except in the broadest possible terms. What in fact exists is a vast melange of subgroups, some categorical, others interacting. Indians of many different tribal origins, Mexican-Americans with innumerable cultural and linguistic backgrounds, Chinese, Japanese, Europeans, Jews, African Americans, are all trying to live together in a single cultural setting. As if this did not present enough difficulties, there is strong class stratification, with each class having its own particular range of cultural behavior.

In stratified societies, power is the name of the game. Each class represents a level of power over the groups lower in the social scale. The wealth and status of the members of any class depend upon using the classes below them. The power structure can be envisioned as the power to control capital goods and finances, power over intellectual skills, and power over physical labor. Power over capital goods prevails over the others because by controlling land, goods, and money, control is maintained over the arena and the means of producing the necessities of life.

Although skills are in themselves valuable, they must be practiced with materials and in localities. The power group controlling the capital goods therefore controls the skills group because it provides the arena for the lawyers, engineers, doctors, and teachers to perform. Those people without capital goods or specialized skills must depend upon the labor of their backs to exist. They either work for themselves, as do native peoples and peasants, or they sell their labor to the classes above them.

Each class tends to develop behavioral patterns that are consistent with the position which it occupies. The ability to determine and affect this behavior is related to the amount of power that each class possesses.

More important than either capital goods or skills is the power to determine the behavior nomemes of the society. What happens in most societies is that some people come to have a determining influence over the nomeme making and nomeme enforcing capacity in a society. This happens in several ways, but one of the most common is during the occurrence of great social change or stress. It is at this time that people are dislocated, their family source of help broken through migration or conquest, or their communication capacity limited because one society becomes dominant over another. It is precisely because of these factors that entrepreneurs like and encourage great dislocating changes since they are more skillful than others at taking advantage of the collapse of existing social structures.

When a group gains control over the nomeme making and enforcing agents of the society, they strive to structure the nomemes to their own advantage. This generally produces both a new kind of society dominated by task and goals concepts, and a different kind of individual. This individual is oriented toward the manipulation of others and of society itself. This manipulation, however, is not for the good of all, but for his private benefit. Society is seen as a captive structure which he uses but to which he does not belong, just as the sheep herder uses and exploits his flock.

Efforts to improve the lot of the lower classes by education and health measure may threaten the position of the higher classes who fully realize they can be displaced if constant vigilance is not maintained. In fact, one of the primary preoccupations of the capital classes is the prevention of members of the lower classes from gaining entrance to their level. This activity takes many direct and indirect forms. The careful structure of the school system, the teacher training programs, the textbook selection, all are vigilantly overseen and designed to maintain the advantage of the capital classes over the middle class and the middle class over the lower class. Schools are deliberately planned to increase the value of the lower class person's labor or skill without enabling him to become a threat to the group above.

Minority groups in America occupy somewhat the same position as do the country's youth in that they are outside the mainstream of national life and the power structure and are blocked from pursuing the same economic, educational, and social activities that the majority enjoy. Often they constitute the lowest social class.

Members of minority groups are almost always distinguishable by such characteristics as skin color, language, clothing, religious practices, or social behavior. These characteristics put the minority person at a double disadvantage. Although an individual's black, brown, or yellow skin is not in itself important, the person is thereby made visible and immediately identifiable to the majority group. Simultaneously, the minority person's physical appearance prompts the members of the majority group to apply behavioral nomemes appropriate to a superior-and-inferior encounter. The prompting occurs because the visible characteristics of the minority person provide clues to expected behavior and responses.

It is not important that the aroused expectations may be erroneous or based upon stereotypes. The fact is, people have preconceptions and when they lack intimate knowledge they use superficial concepts or they take the even easier step of rejecting or acting negatively toward the different person or group. They do so because they are fearful and do not have an adequate base from which to realistically project the behavior of the other individual or group.

Often the appearance of the behavior of the minority group fits the majority culture's concepts of disapproved or unacceptable appearance or behavior. The loud shouting style of some languages strikes people who employ low pitched soft speech as crude and barbaric. Navajo Indians do not respond well to big toothy grins and a gushy type of friendliness. Many

Americans are appalled to discover that their friendliness is not only regarded as not necessarily friendly, but as crude and impolite. Loud boisterous speech contrasts sharply with the almost whispered conversation of the Navajo.

These examples demonstrate that there are many different styles of behavior which contrast strongly with each other and make the position of sub-cultures difficult. None is better or worse than any other. They are merely different and have come into existence for very real purposes. But this does not make contact between members of two different cultural groups easy. On the contrary, it depicts clearly the reality of the problems and the need for profound understanding.

Individualism and Society

In a society like America which is so immense, so impersonal, so unknown and remote, many people begin to reject the concept of a society working for them. They turn to individualism and personal growth for salvation, and thus more easily become the victim of the very system they are trying to escape. They come to believe their condition of despair is the fault of the society, of the culture, when in fact it more often is the result of the emergence of new and different kinds of social situations that demand a new kind of adjustment. In every period of dislocation and breakdown of existing social nomemes, individuals are caught operating with nomemes inappropriate to the situation or are without nomemes at all and are forced back upon biogenic modes of behavior. But the major thrust of every society is toward a working system where all individuals understand and use a common body of cultural plans.

Although man moves toward his destiny through his relationships with others, through his capacity to form and use the power of the group, it is a paradox that man as an individual often rejects society. He strives to break out of the conformity created by the nature of groupness, the very factor that enables him to have a human existence in the first place. He sees the group as restrictive and confining, as preventing the expression of himself, of his uniqueness as an individual. He sees some kind of conflict going on between man, the individual, and a repressive society. The debt each individual owes to his society is not clear. It is too far removed either in time or person for it to mean anything to the individual. He perceives culture as a form of determinism which is a threat to his concept of the individual and free will. He believes he makes his own decisions and is therefore responsible for his own acts. People cause their own growth through their will and through the risk they take. They marry whom they please and are astounded when it does not work out. They have babies and wonder why the child grows up to be such a troublesome person, who causes so much despair and unhappiness. They drink and take drugs and wonder why these are the concern of others. They spend their money on trivia and in their old age have to be supported by welfare. They do all these things in the name of individualism and in the belief that every man chooses his own way and that it is no one else's concern.

But they have failed to understand that culture and society are tools that are intended to work for them. They have missed the message. They do not grasp the fact that when they do not work for society they are working against themselves. They want to use the materials of social life without paying for them, even while they are denying any debt to society.

They do not understand that marriage nomemes exist to make marriage work better, that child-care principles are to enable parents to produce better children, that one can avoid the humiliation of poverty in old age by saving together with others. They only see the imagined restrictions on their imagined freedom.

Personal autonomy may appear to increase as one grows older and more familiar with the cultural alternatives. Freedom is a gradient, narrow and limited as an infant but gradually increasing as one matures. But this is only an appearance, for as one absorbs his culture it tends to become such a part of him that eventually he mistakes the freedom it gives him as his own.

In America, individualism is perpetuated in the schools, in medical care, in the courts and prisons. Few of the personnel working in these institutions can conceive of the groupness of behavior. But individualism is the fruit of the tree, the flowering of the plant of social life, not the seed. For it to exist, to be meaningful, requires a stalk, a trunk, roots and branches, bark and leaves. The kind of fruit that grows, firm and ripe, pithy or sour depends on the tree on which the fruit grows. The tree of human life is the social-cultural system. In the struggle to understand human life people tend to depend upon their own experiences. They project from the nature of their own culture and their own society to all other cultures and societies. But in America this can be a serious mistake. Using America as a standard for understanding human life is as misleading as using a child for understanding the adult. America has neither a culture nor a social structure that provides a means of understanding what societies or cultures are all about. What we see is the bringing together of many different cultures and societies without the emergence of a recognizable functioning unity. Consequently, it is also an error to use the character and personality of an individual American as a model for understanding the person. Both in the case of society and the individual, America is an excellent laboratory to observe the process of cultural and social building. Unfortunately, there is a high rate of failure as shown by the percentage of the population suffering from alcoholism, criminality, and mental and emotional disturbances.

Even the nations of Western Europe offer little better examples because they also have been engaged in a long struggle to create meaningful societies and cultures. The constant wars, famines, epidemics, and vast population movements that have swept Europe for the past 1500 years have continuously disrupted the formation of workable social institutions. Again there is a paradox. For the very struggle and disruption, the uncertainty and danger, forced man into a creativity that he might not otherwise have obtained. Seeking ways of surviving, European man invented new forms of marriage, new architecture, new machinery, new political structures, new arts and music. He set out upon long journeys and discovered the world. He became more aware of himself through his discovery of others. He found new products and new markets. He was forced out of his old cultural mold and into the creation of a new.

From this process American society arose, and from the experience of America, a whole new dimension to human existence is gradually emerging. But it is far from clear what the structure of this new life will be like, for already it is encountering the realities of global existence, the overpopulation threat, the startling depletion of natural resources. The struggle is no longer between tribes or even nations but between segments of the globe as new alignments replace old, and technological inventions tie all the world together.

CHAPTER NINE

CULTURE, LANGUAGE AND COMMUNICATION

The essence of any society, however simple or sophisticated, is the commonality of behavior its members share. If behavior is largely determined by cognitive or nomemic instructions then some mechanism must exist which transmits these nomemes from person to person throughout the group. Broadly speaking this mechanism is communication.

Culture is related to language and communication in much the same way it is related to other aspects of behavior. It provides the self instructions to create the form of expression as well as the means for interpretation. That is, nomemes provide the instructions for creating the communication elements, whether gestures or sound, as well as the rules for understanding the meaning of the gestures or sound. Speech presents a special situation, for not only does it make possible the verbal exchange of data and ideas but it also gives an individual an internal mental language with which to manipulate his cognitive processes.

Communication, however, is not confined to humans. It occurs everywhere throughout the biological world. All living things are in sensory contact with the environment around them and are communicating with that world. But it is communication at a relatively low level. It lacks the intentionality, the information, the structure and regularity of higher level communication found in human societies. Human communication is characterized by goals and purpose. It can be both informative and manipulative, and usually includes a conscious and purposeful exchange of information. It provides the means of sharing and activating cultural nomemes for the purpose of bringing about change and adjustments in human life.

The basic modes of communicating among humans are visual, auditory, and tactile. Gestures, postures, shapes, movements, colors, and relationships between things and events which can be observed all communicate when there are nomemes of activation and nomemes for interpretation available. Body language, dance, art, and sculpture also communicate through the nomenic structure they represent.

What one hears also communicates. Even the simplest auditory activity such as body noise, pounding the fist, stamping the feet, snapping the fingers, conveys a message. More specific meanings are provided by the non-systematic sounds of groans, grunts, sighs, and moans. Systematic employment and arrangement of sounds through more elaborate nomemic patterns eventuates in true speech with an increasing percentage of symbols and abstractions and a high degree of information content.

Touching is another way of communicating. Feeling the shape of an object, testing its weight or its texture, are direct and sensitive means of acquiring information provided the nomemes are available for interpreting this sensory information. Caressing a lover transmits feelings and concepts not possible by any other means.

Auditory communication is a special kind of interpersonal contact that is largely dependent upon two unusual biological characteristics of humans, a complex flexible vocal apparatus and a correspondingly complex auditory mechanism. Speech activity includes the person who sends out vocal signals according to some pattern of nomemes he has learned and the person who receives these sounds and possesses the nomemic code for translating them into cognitive understanding.

All vocal sounds need not be speech, however, and they need not be language, just as all languages are not vocal.

Speech differs from all other forms of communication in that it has a far greater symbolic and abstract quality, and it depends upon a vast complex nomemic infrastructure or grammar. It is not necessarily dependent upon events and objects in the immediate landscape. Man can discuss events of long ago or far away as easily as he can things in front of him. The chosen symbols and signals are arbitrary and become fixed only as a result of repeated implementation of particular nomemes within a speech group.

The acquisition of communication skills in growing individuals is not random and accidental. There is an order and sequence in the process which is correlated with the general physical maturation of the child. It is closely related to the daily needs of the person and to his ability to grasp relationships and to generalize. The order in terms of maturation is tactile, visual, and auditory.

The infant first begins to learn about the world through touch, the primary and fundamental sensory process. Sensitivity is present at the birth of the infant; the skin is the basic organ, receiving and transmitting a multitude of messages. Infant animals respond to and are activated by the touching, licking, and nuzzling of others. Touching and being touched enables the newborn to orient themselves and begin the basic process of developing the nomemes for unraveling the world around them and for responding to that world.

In the human infant, being handled is soon extended to handling, to active exploration through the hand and fingers. The infant becomes more aware of himself by feeling his own body, by moving his arms and legs, by kicking and grasping. These movements lead to nomemes for coordinating his movements and for understanding what he feels. He gradually comes to realize what he is, and to understand what he is like relative to other objects in the world around him. He constructs nomemes that tell him some things are hard and hurtful and others soft and pleasurable.

These tactile experiences of the infant shape much of his initial concepts of the world, of himself, and of others. Touching does not cease as the child grows older, but changes as his social contacts enlarge and he learns that different kinds and forms of touching are encouraged or discouraged in the society. Every society either directly or indirectly establishes nomemes relating to the kinds and degrees of permitted and prohibited touching. In some, people are not inclined to permit others to touch them and get physically close. In others, touching and physical closeness are encouraged and rewarded. Communicating between people of two such opposing concepts about touch can produce many misunderstandings and conflict because each society considers its way to be correct and the other way to be wrong.

Visual communication between humans transmits both information and emotional states and includes a vast repertoire of gestures and body activity. Facial, hand, arm, body, and eye gestures are all employed. These are used even at the lower primate level where an old baboon suddenly freezing to stare intently over the veldt is quickly understood and responded to by the members of the group.

Attempting to read human gestures can be misleading and dangerous because they appear so natural and obvious. Serious conflicts often arise in cross cultural situations because people interpret body communication in terms of their own society and culture. But like other aspects of communication, body language can only be correctly understood by possessing the nomemes for interpreting particular gestures and movements.

For example, such a simple thing as a head nod may carry entirely different meanings. When people in America wish to signify "yes" the nomeme is to move the head up and down, but in Turkey the nomeme for "yes" is down only, while moving the head up means "no." In America one shrugs his shoulders and head to indicate indecision, indefinite, or not knowing, but a Turk nods his head from side to side to convey these ideas.

In America, people in general tend to convey their feelings by their facial expression. They smile when they are friendly or happy and frown when they are unhappy, but people in other societies often maintain an expressionless face and do not reveal their feelings by their facial appearance. They realize that others can read their emotional state through their facial expression and may gain an advantage over them in an interpersonal encounter, consequently they tend to reduce facial communication to a minimum.

In some Mediterranean countries, speech and gestures often appear violent, angry, and quarrelsome to other people. The shouting speech, the wild gestures all convey anger, but in fact it is merely the normal manner of conversing.

Man created speech. He invented words, sentences, and concepts. They were not lying about waiting to be plucked, packaged, and labeled like fruit on a tree. He created them out of the innate capacity of his brain, of his vocal tools, out of the keenness of his hearing, and from the channels that connect the two, hidden deep in the complexities of the mind. So while the particulars are arbitrary, the agreements among the members of a speech group are not, since the success of communication is totally dependent upon these agreements. Man does more than signal alarms, sound fears, and express joys. He adds details of size, shape, distance, and bearing, but the communication of these is directly related to the acceptance and mutual understanding of the speech elements, the sounds, words, and meanings used.

It is very clear from examining primate and human communication processes that two different things are involved. These two things are directly related to the separation of emotion and cognition. Primate communication expresses largely affective states and relatively little cognitive data. Apes and monkeys can communicate only a minimum of information. Humans on the other hand can transmit both emotional states and information and--even more profound--data about their emotional states. Man conveys his ideas, his feelings, his fears to others. He releases a flood of words that transmits a never ending cascade of thought and emotion. He relates what is present and what is not present, that which is near and that which is long past. He creates a world where concepts and symbols perform an intricate and dazzling dance limited only by the meanings he gives them.

The general process by which a child acquires a speech appears to be universal, a basic human capacity. Although the precise age at which a child is ready for or makes a developmental step is not the same for every individual, the general pattern is similar. The fundamental basis for speech acquisition is the ability to recognize, categorize, and mimic sounds. In speech there are two factors: the ability to hear words, that is, a series of arbitrary sounds that form an auditory unit, and the ability to vocalize words. The auditory processes in humans are directly connected to the speech process so that man can reproduce the sounds that he hears. This capability is limited in other animals, including the higher primates.

The learning of speech appears to be a formidable task, yet the infant is not daunted. He sets about immediately upon birth to accomplish this end, a tiny creature struggling with a vast deluge of sights and sounds, determined, and almost always successful. He appears to receive little help. His struggle is internal but he is prepared, and, unwittingly, he receives the necessary assistance. He must hear, and he must make sounds. He applies to language acquisition the same procedure for constructing nomemes he employs with all other aspects of behavior, the same as any complex animal uses, but far more extensively.

The sequence of language learning has many regularities. The auditory and vocal systems go through a series of growth or developmental stages, which are closely tied to the general growth and maturation of the brain. As the child ages chronologically he reaches different stages of readiness. Each stage enables him to be responsive to a different aspect of the auditory stimulus occurring around him. All children, regardless of race or nationality, seem equally capable of making the full range of human sounds. All begin with an initial trial and error period, followed by the application of selected nomemes developed during this experimentation. Language is not acquired by simply memorizing a set of grammatical rules and a list of words. It is acquired by developing a set of nomemes which one can apply to create and interpret sounds.

During the first few weeks or months of life the infant exercises his vocal apparatus and attunes his ear, but he is already noting and responding to the auditory regularities that he hears. At first this response is very simple and awkward, but as he continues to experience the world of sound he gradually improves his nomemic control over his vocal production. He begins with crying and wailing but soon adds cooing. He does not replace crying but simply adds new sounds. Soon he has developed the nomemes that enable him to discriminate between sounds and to recognize recurring noises. He internalizes and synthesizes these nomemes and eventually identifies the source and concommitant activity associated with each sound. He is ready for the next stage of development. After the fourth or fifth month he stops cooing and moves on to more speech-like behavior. His experiments may appear to produce only random noise but he is attempting to make sounds in response to what he hears. He repeats more and more of the sounds that occur in his parent language. As he floats out this babble of noise, some receive more regular and meaningful response from other persons, and he constructs a nomeme to take this into account. These sounds he tends to repeat, and slowly he builds up a body of self instructions that enables him to control the movements of his tongue, lips and voice box and to determine the individual sounds that he makes.

By the time he is nine to twelve months old he begins to regularize his sound making and ceases to babble. He no longer experiments with the total range of sounds but has begun to concentrate upon a few, those that he will eventually use in this native language. He makes more and more sounds that are distinct vowels and consonants. He is increasingly aware that he can change the sound that he makes and that different sounds produce different responses from the world around him.

Before the end of the first year the child has developed a vast series of nomemes that enable him to produce the dozen or so basic sounds that he needs to construct the words that he normally will use. The fact that there seems to be some order in this process is only a reflection of the order found in his culture, in the basic trial and error process, and in his physical maturation. If the nomemes the child builds for himself coincide with the nomemes of his language group, it is not because he innately knows the language but because those around him help shape what he hears by their response. Those responses correspond to the nomemes of that language. Through many thousands of random efforts, untold trial and error explorations, similarities and duplications occur, are recognized and are organized into a language system, but it is always the language of the child's culture and no other that emerges.

The child now begins to comprehend the concept of labeling or naming. Whereas before he has had vague and generalized concepts, he now comes to realize that different objects can be distinguished and labeled with a particular sound. Naming is reinforced by the adults around him and soon he has a name concept for many objects. He constructs nomemes indicating that certain sounds are related to certain objects and events. He sees this as a regularity and even comes to realize that things for which he does not yet have a name nevertheless do have a label.

It is not long before he also realizes that there are two types of naming words, those that name objects and those that name action. He learns the object names first but soon he grasps the second concept. Once he distinguishes between the two types of naming words, he becomes aware that the name objects are what have action. He can make the object act by attaching an action word to it; dog run, run dog. He may put the action word before or after the object word but he seeks to construct rules or regularity in how he orders the words he uses.

When the child reaches eighteen months of age, he will begin to assimilate the basic structure of his language, a task he will continue for several years more. He has now acquired a considerable list of nomemes that name objects and name actions. He struggles with the difficult task of learning how to put different types of words together into longer grammatical utterances. In the beginning he does not always use the existing grammar of the language, but constructs his own out of his experience and of his inherent capacity to see order and regularity. Gradually the grammar of his language emerges.

Once he grasps the grammatical or nomemes pattern, he then seeks new words to substitute for old words and begins to greatly expand the size of his vocabulary and the length and complexity of his utterances. This mighty task is well on the way to completion by the time he is three years old.

What the child hears is crucial not only for learning language, but for providing the requirements upon which brain organization is dependent. The initial sound-hearing and sound-making activities are brain training exercises. Random sounds, irregular responses, and inefficient auditory experiences, inhibit the development of the neurological pathways and connections vital to adult thinking and speaking. There is protection against this since the infant can determine some of the sounds he hears by controlling the sounds he himself makes. Total deprivation is therefore difficult, but partial deprivation is ever present.

In an irregular world, in a world without regularities and repetitions, the child will not find the order necessary for the construction of usable nomemes. Giving a child random nonsense sounds, baby talk, too many dialects, or too many languages, obscure the regularities he depends upon and seeks. The cognitive pathways and nomemes that he develops at these stages are those he is going to use to understand and to deal with the world at future stages. If he hears a language style that is social and affective, but low in information content, this is the material he has to work with. If he does not hear analytical or expository language then he fails to develop the capacities required by this language style to the extent children who have heard these uses do. He cannot wait. At each stage of his linguistic growth he is dependent upon his environment for the materials that permit that stage to be fulfilled. Only by special training can he come back later and make up what he may have missed or misunderstood.

Language has a unique position in the theory of culture. As a fundamental cultural development it stands alongside other human inventions such as tools, art, or social structure. But language is more, for it is not only a special cultural attribute in itself but is the agent that transmits much of the remaining cultural inventory from person to person. Furthermore, it is a tool that is not confined solely to intracommunication activities but vastly expands consciousness and self-awareness by enabling the individual to communicate with himself at a complex level.

Since language is the means by which worldly information becomes cultural it is not surprising then that the nature of the language used begins to take an active part in the kind of information received and the manner in which it is interpreted. The senses are not merely automatic passive organs; they develop and sharpen their various capacities through training and experience. This training and practice is largely conducted in cultural terms through the mechanics of language or speech. Thus this process is circular in that what one sees influences the original language or cultural form, but once a language becomes an operational tool, it influences what one sees and how one interprets what one sees. Many people are unaware of the influence of language on their existence. They believe that what they do and say is a product of their own special personality, of their own intrinsic style. They believe all languages essentially are neutral in the process of thinking and expressing, acting only as a mediator. They are unaware of the impact of the language struc-ture itself on their thinking and behavior. But a language through the structural arrangement of its conceptual units, its sequential order, and its grammat-ical categories, is inserted directly into the behavioral stream. It is not passive in its influence. The linguistic treatment of time, space, shape, action, and the emphasis given to the material or subjective aspects of existence, conditions the way the language user perceives and interprets the world and his rela-tionship to it. This conditioning produces a consistent and internalized manner of interpreting life, a world view. This world view is not shaped by language alone but by the nature of the external world, and by that segment of it which any individual experiences.

World view refers to the general stance or position one takes toward certain aspects of human existence. World views held by individuals are not static but grow and emerge as the individual biologically ages and increases the totality of his life experience. What is huge and menacing to a child may greatly diminish in size as the child grows older. What seems far away and distant to a young boy may seem quite near a few years later. But at any given age the world view is the device which by its own peculiar qualities colors the sensory input.

The world view of an individual is analogous to a radio with its station selector, tone modulator, and volume control. Each setting enables the listener to receive only one channel or program even though many programs may fill the air simultaneously. What one hears and how one hears it is determined and limited to the particular station one is tuned to. Life and language create many programs but the individual's culture and language setting, like the radio receiver, selects out only certain things to reach the listener.

The world view is the distinctive and particular way of perceiving time, space, matter, and the energy system activating the universe. It refers to the overt and covert philosophical and cosmological principles of a cultural system which the individual absorbs through his language and social experience. An individual's world view affects his behavior because it acts as a monitor between the biological activity of sensing and the cognitive process of recognition, evaluation labeling, and reacting.

The universe can be perceived in many dimensions and the dimensions each individual receives and responds to is determined by how he is cognitively organized. If one wears blue tinted glasses, the world may look blue. To one who wears green it may appear green. If one reverses a pair of binoculars the world shrinks; and if one is partially deaf the world's cacophony is muted. Because everyone has ears and eyes does not mean that everyone hears and sees the same things in the same way. What one hears is what one is trained to hear and what one sees depends upon what one has learned to see. World view refers to the cognitive framework which one uses to evaluate the product on his senses, and the manner in which one evaluates his sensory input affects the way he will respond.

In its simplest aspect world view is concerned with the concepts of time and space. It serves as a constant reference model for evaluation, judging, and understanding what is transpiring. It provides the measure for making choices and for determining likenesses and opposition. It emphasizes a particular concept of time, whether a discrete measurable units like railroad cars along a track, a flow like a river, or an atmosphere neither linear, flowing nor unitized.

Distance, location, and space can be viewed in many ways, as relative, as infinite, as regular or random, or as a product of the intensity of emotional response. The measured mile to the top of Mount Everest is not the same mile on the Olympic track, a dying man's crawl for help is far different than the wedding march. The hour of boredom at a bus station is not the same as the sixty minutes before an execution. Life may appear short if happy, long if unhappy.

The way of viewing these events directly affects how one behaves. The arctic winter with its three months of semi-darkness, its blistering wind, and fifty-below temperatures paralyzes the measurer of hours and minutes.

World view does not refer to the behavior itself but to those factors that shape the perceptual input. The flow of mental processes then begins with behavioral activity in the external world, becomes an evaluation of the sensory response determined by the individual's world view, and eventuates in the selection of a cultural plan for action, and response. World view then is that composite instrument in the mental process that provides a consistent base for the interpretation of received sensory data.

This base is somewhat different in different cultures. If one is an American he perceives the size of automobiles differently from a European. A Volkswagen is seen as a small car, a Ford as medium sized and a Cadillac as large. When an American first arrives in Italy, almost all cars are seen as small and some such as the Fiat as mini. It is difficult to imagine getting into one of these tiny vehicles or trying to drive them. They are hard to take seriously and one may even try to kick them out of his path as he might a toy. Gradually, however, as one stays longer, the concept of size changes until it is realized that the Volkswagen is really a medium sized car, the Fiat is the small car, and the Cadillac is not large but monstrous. Then when one returns to America all the cars seem very large and gross until one gradually readjusts his vision again.

How one perceives himself relative to the size of other people can be effected in the same way. An American man or woman of slightly above average stature is nothing exceptional in the United States. But in southern Europe they may feel like giants as they look out over the heads of both men and women.

In a sense then these are altered states of awareness produced by the basic world view. How one reacts or behaves toward others may be influenced by how one reacts to relative size. A tall robust American woman may find it difficult to take a short slight Italian romeo seriously. American men are constantly aware of the appearance factor when dealing with others. A male responds to a girl he perceives as beautiful far differently than he does toward a woman he perceives as ordinary.

How does a world view become established as a fundamental cognitive base? World view encompasses not only the physiological and perceptual processes but the language which the individual uses to cognitively interpret and manage the perceptual information that he receives.

Most of the qualities of space, time, and energy by which objects are distinguished and identified, are properties given to them by man. They are not intrinsic in the objects themselves. A Cadillac is neither large or small by itself but its size is a quality given by the viewer which is linguistically labeled. Language is the basic medium of world view because it provides both the word tools with which to identify percepts, and the structural arrangements by which words go beyond naming and begin to characterize the world more fully.

Language is not merely a recording and transmitting device that faithfully reproduces some separate external reality. For humans, language is the reality. To the biologist, a horse is a particular species of mammal; to the cowboy, he is a form of transportation; to early man, a good juicy steak; to the fourteen year old girl, a love object . . what the horse is depends upon who is doing the viewing.

The number and kinds of words available in one's vocabulary may limit or expand one's perception of some experience and the ability to think and communicate. To the cowboy, the word horses may mean very little. His vocabulary includes far more precise terms such as stallion, mare, colt yearling, mustang, bay, pinto, swayback, stud, hammerhead, roman rose and so forth. The person without these terms conceives vaguely and communicates vaguely. He does not know or grasp the connotation of hammerhead, yearling or thoroughbred.

In the same way one cannot share the connisseur's appreciation of a good wine unless he has developed the capacity to distinguish between and identify red and white wines, dry and sweet wines, good years and bad. The connoisseur's view of wine is vastly different from that of the occasional sipper, and he has developed a vocabulary that enables him to mentally deal with concepts that are unknown to the nondrinker.

The morphological structures of language and its relationship to world view is more subtle, less obvious and more difficult to demonstrate than the lexical. This refers primarily to the placement in a sentence of various concepts represented by words, suffixes, prefixes, and accents. To say, "I am going to town"; places a far stronger emphasis on the actor than a sentence such as, "Going to town am I"; where the emphasis is on the act of going. Different languages, by the placement of the various parts of speech, influence how the listener perceives the focus of the sentence. Some American Indian languages have few if any time orienting markers such as past, present, and future tense endings. They express time differently, but the tense-structured languages by their constant emphasis on locating events relative to time, force the user to adapt a certain stance in their thinking and speaking about time. It cannot be ignored if one wishes to use those languages.

Navajo language forces a certain kind of reality upon the user. Rather than modifying the verb to represent different aspects of time, Navajo uses verbs according to some quality of the object of the action. Thus different verbs might be used for the same action but with objects of different quality. The verb used to denote throwing a stick would be different from the verb used to denote throwing a ball, and still different for throwing a snake. Furthermore, the selection of the verb would also be related to several other factors such as the sex of the person doing the throwing. Thus the speakers of this language may not pay much attention to the time or date an event occurred, but they pay very close attention to the quality of the objects

involved. Again, this is not merely an idiosyncrasity
or oddity, but is clearly reflected in how the Navajo
see the world and how they react to it. For example,
it has often been noted that Navajo have remarkable
memory for detail and a basic characteristic of their
art work is the minute detail and clarity with which
they draw. The important factor about world view is
the direction a basic principle sets for response and
behavior. Fundamental principles or world views in
different societies are often highly contrastive and
opposing. They cannot easily be reconciled. It is
difficult for one to hold that the world is both mechan-
istic and animate, rational and supernatural, that an
automobile is both large and small, or that something
is both near and far.

The effect of language upon the user is unique for
each language and in many ways difficult, if not
impossible, to translate from one language to another.
Some languages have a paucity of noun words and
emphasize verbal forms which presents the world as
being in process rather than static the way English
often does. The Mayan languages are heavy with words
which indicate spatial awareness, but they have few
temporal indicators. Every utterance is full of forms
describing where the speaker is in space, where other
objects are, whether someone is near or far. Direc-
tionals indicate which way one is going, how far, and
if one is going once, occasionally, or over and over
again. The speakers, therefore, constantly visualize
a spatial world where everything is precisely located,
and the direction of things relative to each other are
already noted. Speakers are lost without these kinds
of locators. They have difficulty understanding instructions or folk stories without them. Perhaps because of
the steep mountains and dense jungle growth, it was
necessary to create mental and verbal maps of the
topography to keep from getting lost and to keep track
of each other. The language builds into the child a
constant reminder to know where one is and not to
wander away.

English, on the other hand, tends to be more

concerned with locating people and events relative to time--the past, the present and future. English verbs are structured to signify time through tense forms. Other people such as the Navaho, Maya, or Trobrianders do not structure temporal qualities in the same way and tend to ignore the past, present, future continuum. They focus on present being, the now.

English and other European languages ascribe a high degree of reality to abstract and subjective words which enable these words to be treated as manipulative objects. This characteristic produces many spurious metaphysical arguments and discussions, questions which may appear totally incomprehensible to persons from a different language background where such questions might never occur. Merely because it is possible to construct questions which are grammatically correct and which have the appearance of reality does not make them real to other people. Many of the great problems in Western philosophy are questions of this nature. They were language problems, not universal problems.

Languages vary in their use of command or coercive styles. English is replete with forms which are means of imposing one person's will over another's: 'go', 'come', 'do', 'eat', 'shut up', permeate the language. But such coercive expressions are not necessarily universal. They are merely a product of the particular language used. Some languages have few of these forms although this does not mean their speakers have no method of commanding when necessary. The usual way of getting someone to do what you want them to is more circuitous, subtle, and polite. Many American Indian cultures do not reward coercion or demanding, commanding persons or actions. Imposing one's will on someone or something else is foreign to the culture. Animals manage themselves, and humans do not need to be directed. Inanimate objects require a different treatment. While one cannot make a horse run, one can move a rock. This concept has wide implications. Indian parents tend not to order their children but to guide or assist them or show them the way, a quite different approach from that usual in America. To the Indian, one does not have the right to impose one's will on someone else, a view supported by the language structure which has a paucity of coercive forms.

Internal communication in humans presents a special problem because of its subjective nature. In animals, internal feeling states are apt to be translated directly into external action patterns and the interpretation of the emotion is the action which results. But in humans, feeling states often go through one or more intermediate stages before they result in action. One must learn to identify the feeling state as anger or fear or love, and it is not necessary to deal with the feeling state directly for one can substitute the name word for the feeling. Thus some people with overdeveloped recognition capacities interpret every mild feeling state as a major event because they have the capacity to recognize and label it. Many people are confused by this capacity, mistaking the label for the reality. Labeling a feeling state neither alters it or makes it more real, though it enables one to manipulate the label and to communicate with oneself or with others. But unfortunately, the reality of the label cannot be verified by others.

Language--communication--has itself gone through a series of historical and developmental stages. These are closely related to technological inventions and the recent extension of the human voice through electronics. In the beginning a person was restricted in his communication efforts by the limits of his vocal power. Thus much communication was bounded by the distance the voice would carry and the number of people who were in range of that voice. Communication was a face to face situation where there was the immediate presence of both a speaker and a listener. The nomemes of interpersonal communication took full note of this condition.

It was not until the written message came into existence that man was able to communicate extensively beyond the immediate situation and to convey a message over great distances or across time periods. In face to face communication the emotional content of the message is directly and physically felt, whereas in the written word there is no immediate physical confrontation between sender and receiver. Anger that in the first instance might turn to deadly violence was no immediate threat when read a hundred miles away or years later. Even with the development of the radio or telephone one was relatively immune to the immediate consequences of the message. As a result of these technological inventions, a new kind of boldness or attitude in interpersonal behavior developed where things could now be thought and said that freed the writer or reader from the fear of physical retaliation or immediate decisions. Physically weaker persons could engage in behavior that would have been unthinkable in a direct confrontation situation. Problems became more abstract and detached, for reading about a murder is not the same thing as being physically present no matter how graphically described.

With the advent of the film and television all this was again changed. Once more there is the immediate physical and visual presence, although simulated, so that again one can see and hear the action or the crime. But there is a significant difference, for while a murder is seen and heard, it is not really present, so one can lounge comfortably in his overstuffed chair, sipping a cold beverage and watch on the screen, quite detachedly, the most appalling activities without the slightest real danger.

This creates an unreal world where children one minute can see a gun fired and someone killed, but the very next hour see the victim on another program cheery and healthy as if nothing had happened to him at all. They may sit placidly by watching their parents engage in a violent quarrel thinking they are watching another scene from the latest domestic comedy on television. Thus this form of communication builds still another world view, one with all the sound and shadow of reality but without substance. Furthermore it enables nomemes to be constructed which are entirely inappropriate and misleading in real life.

Human behavior is totally involved with communication. Speech as one form of communication is a special and distinctive tool of man, yet it is not a passive tool such as an axe or a spear, but by its own structure affects the user in important and unsuspected ways. It illustrates the nomemic structure of culture in a way that few other aspects of culture can.

CHAPTER TEN

BECOMING A PERSON

Everyone must learn to be who he is. No one is born a person. There is only the potential for humanness, a potential that must be nurtured and cared for, shaped and molded before it reaches realization. To become human does not mean some miraculous unfolding of innate qualities of goodness, well being and love, or aggression or hate. There is no preformation of these traits in anyone. To become human means to become enculturated with the substance of the cultural system in which one lives.

Every individual arrives in an existing cultural world, a world that has already formed and structured most things in life. There are many cultural worlds, each vastly different, and each producing different kinds of people. While all humans have a similar biological heritage, each emerging person has a cultural experience that shapes him in a unique way. The preformation of personality traits and behavior, therefore, does not occur within the individual but rather within the content and structure of the cultural system. The human body is a crucible and an agent into which are poured life experiences and from which will emerge a human being. But a person is never completed, never finalized. He is always learning and growing, forgetting and dying. An individual is one thing as an infant, another as a child, and quite another as an adult.

Learning the cultural system, learning the nomemes of one's society, means learning what other people already know, what they have already structured and ordered, what they have abstracted from their contact with the experiental world. From the process of coping with that world, each person struggles to grasp the regularities and recurrences of life and projects them into a guidance system. It is this guiding system of nomemes that the child learns, and which transforms him into a human being.

There are many ways to learn, although all are in the end dependent upon the same fundamental neuro-logical processes. Whatever the learning system, the goal is the same, and that is the acquisition of a body of nomemes which will enable the individual to function effectively in his society.

Learning the culture of one's group is not neces-sarily dependent upon teaching. The most widely used and successful learning occurs rather through observa-tion and imitation. Observation is usually followed by a trial and error period of imitation, experimentation in which one tries out what one has observed.

Teaching, that is, supervised and directed learning, is neither the most common or the most successful learning method. While all societies may use some teaching, the vast majority of learning occurs in other ways. It is only in certain societies that teaching has become synonomous with learning and where a vast teaching infrastructure in the form of schools and instructors has developed.

Teaching in general is closely associated with verbalization, that is, one person telling another some-thing through language. Observation and imitation on the other hand is essentially nonverbal. Much more may be involved here than merely different learning techniques, for verbal skills often form an intervening element between the teacher and the learner. The learner and the teacher must be on the same verbal wave lengths before meaningful learning can occur and very often they are not. Furthermore verbal and non-verbal learning may be somewhat different forms of learning since verbal learning seems to be primarily located in the left hemisphere of the brain and non-verbal learning in the right hemisphere. To have skill in one type of learning does not necessarily imply skill in the other.

The learning process is more than just an isolated event in a person's life. It is a continuous activity in which what one has already learned strongly influences what one will learn. Each new segment of learning requires a threshold of prior knowledge. It is as if one were going up a set of stairs, each level reached making it possible to take the next step. One's learning experience is like walking across a field full of large boulders. As one approaches each boulder he goes around it. The direction one takes around the obstruction determines what obstacle he will encounter next and which new change in direction he will take. The way he reacts to each obstacle then, determines which subsequent set of problems he will have to solve. Although in the end he presumably will get across the field, his exact path will show many zigs and zags in direction, each subsequent detour or change in route being influenced to an extent by his previous choices. At the same time, he is acquiring experiences which shape his next choice of direction as he proceeds farther and farther across the field.

Just as every step the traveler takes influences his future, so every day in the life of the newborn, every moment is important. It is important because each experience is a step in the construction of a nomeme that will relate to the next event, the next happening. The first events of life are forgotten, are never remembered in detail. But the chain of experience begins building nomemes, one link after another. Nothing is left out, nothing ignored. The first hand that holds the child, the first words that he hears are important. Because touch is the primary medium, the nature and amount of touch, its regularity, its gentleness or roughness, is vital as a stimulant and as a clue to the world beyond. It conditions the infant's first nomemes about feeling, of sensing. Already he seeks regularity, in touching, in sounds, in handling, struggling to make sense of the world. He has many built-in regularities: hunger, thirst, breathing, feeding, changing, tossing and turning. The child develops nomemes of expectancy from the person who manages these things for him, the mother or nurse, not because he has some quantity of love he must give to someone, but because he has a need for grasping the nature of the world into which he has been introduced. He responds to regularity, but irregularity frustrates and inhibits his growth. Changes in the persons who handle him, in how they handle him, in what he is exposed to, do not enable him to develop his capacity for constructing nomemes that makes order of the world.

The regularity he perceives must be in keeping with his immediate comfort needs as well as his bodily functions. Irregular feeding, feeding out of time with his biological rhythms, prevent the development of nomemes that provide him with an orderly grasp of the life experience. If he cannot make meaningful nomemes of what is going on he may turn off, become apathetic, frustrated or autistic. Sudden changes in the regular way of doing things, of the expected way of handling, cause irreparable damage to the chain of order that he is developing.

Imagine creating a wire mobile hanging from the ceiling. One begins at the top and link by link adds downward a wire here, a figure there until the structure is finished. If a link is incorrectly made or left out then all that follows will be affected. The chain the infant is constructing is closely influenced by his innate maturation process. Each link must occur in the right order and close to the proper time in the general growth pattern because what a child needs at any particular stage of his growth is critical to his continued development.

The maturation process is powerful. It occurs independently of ordinary obstacles. It is a biological pre-programming and its force is such that even congenitally deaf children go through the gurgling, babbling stages at the same time a normal child does. But there is a difference, for the deaf child who cannot hear his own noise makes fewer total sounds and is slower in putting a series of sounds together. He, of course, has difficulty making words and sentences. Without an auditory experience the child cannot make full use of his maturation growth. This does not mean that he does not struggle to communicate. He learns other techniques, body gestures and hand movements to express himself. And these expressions occur at the same time in his growth cycle as they would if he could hear. Children who have been restricted from walking nevertheless will try to walk at much the same age as other children do. These regularities are provided by the biological system.

Children in foster homes or institutions do not languish because they lack love or affection, but because they cannot develop the nomemes of an orderly world view as a result of the type of handling and growth limiting experience which they receive. These experiences are often repetitious and non-progressive and the child cannot attach to any particular person any expectation of regularity. Nurses and caretakers are always changing and while there may be a clock routine. this is not sufficient for the development of the child. Failure to receive the necessary experience at the appropriate point in the maturation process means there is a gap in the emotional and neural growth which is often irreparable. Just as muscles must be exercised, and just as a person cannot lift one hundred pounds until he has lifted ninety, so the neural structures of the brain must have opportunities to grow that are in accord with the inherent patterns of maturation.

New kinds of experiences are useful and necessary for human growth but their value is of a different order. They enlarge the scope of the child's world, but they must be congruent with the design the child has already begun in his mind. They must be capable of being fitted into the world view which the child is working hard to develop.

While the infant lies in his crib seemingly idle, great events are taking place. Far from being helpless and apathetic, the child's mind is gathering and ordering each little fragment of sensory experience, shaping and molding it into nomemes that will provide a consistent whole from which he will project his next experience. Denied this opportunity the child cannot develop a meaningful world picture and will not develop an adequate stage from which to attack the next problem.

From the very instant of birth, then, the child is subject to enculturation, to socialization, to learning. He learns the facts of his culture and he learns about the people who carry that culture. He begins to learn the nomemes by which the people in his life-sphere operate, how they deal with objects, with time, with the bodily functions. He learns the rules of social behavior, of how people treat and mistreat each other. Enculturation establishes within the individual the set of operating nomemes to be used as guides for acting in particular behavioral settings. It is not enough simply to know about the cultural nomemes. The individual must reach the point where he operates almost automatically or habitually from these internalized cultural instructions that he possesses.

This process occurs in many ways, in subtle non-apparent happenings. Play and children's games are an important way that a child learns about nomemes, and consequently the peer group is a primary source of enculturation and socialization. This is an ancient primate characteristic and the play learning of chimpanzees and baboons is surprisingly similar to children's activity. Here the child responds to sounds, movements, and feelings by imitating and mimicking older children's behavior often without understanding the reasons for some particular act. They may be instructed directly by other children and are rewarded and punished by the group so that an element of direct training is involved. From this they learn concentration and attention to detail, muscular coordination and roles and social status, which are imitative of future adult behavior.

Closely related to structured learning are ritual and ceremony. Ritual learning is both imitative and repetitive.

Trial and error is also basic to the overall learning process. Animals well below the primate level learn by trying different solutions and rejecting those that are not successful. Monkeys and apes solve quite complicated matters given enough time and incentive. They even have the mental capacity to retain and recall solutions from one situation to the next. Children go about understanding the world in a similar trial and error fashion, exploring, probing, accepting, rejecting.

Animals act out of their own individual private experience. Each develops his own catalogue of useful information which he has culled from his trial and error activities. Only a limited amount of his experience can be transferred to other animals although this is much more than was once suspected. Humans, however, have developed extensive methods for sharing their trials and their errors, enabling solutions to be cumulative. Man has shortened the experimental learning process of each individual by feeding the residual of many people's learning into a single person's life stream. Nevertheless each individual continues to apply trial and error evaluation even to the cultural material he is exposed to, evaluating it and fitting it to his own experience.

Trial and error involves activity doing and testing. It is one thing to watch a man perform a skilled act, but quite another to replicate that act. While a person can achieve a certain understanding or mastery of behavior merely from watching and discussing, the test comes in the attempt to actually perform. The novice, even with step by step instructions, may still not be able to achieve until he has developed in his mind a clear, precise mental prototype of the behavioral acts involved in an episode. Of course it is possible for activity to take place when the mental image is uncertain and unclear, but the behavior will show uncertainty and the result will not be what he desired.

Nomemes and images do not occur miraculously in

the mind because they are desired. A mental image develops in relation to the clarity of the instructions or of the observation. It is strengthened and further clarified by careful practice and self examination. Persons who are learning new tasks without clear nomemes, stumble around through a hit and miss process. Occasionally, they chance upon solutions which appear to be satisfactory, but often they are not pleased, knowing that other people are more accomplished than they. If they seek formal coaching or teaching, they often find it hard or impossible to eradicate and change the habit patterns they have already internalized. Children constantly have this problem. They have developed the wrong images and nomemes of behavior. They copy older children who have learned incorrectly. They imitate parents and relatives who have learned informally.

The greatest lessons come from athletics. Not only have human performances improved dramatically in recent years, but the total number of individuals who now exceed former achievements is incredible. Before the application of rational formal methods of training arose, occasional individuals excelled through some fortunate accident of private discovery or exceptional talent. With the accumulation and sharing of rational techniques and training methods, vast numbers of people have discovered abilities they never dreamed existed. The potential of the human being has far exceeded the wildest speculation. It has been made possible by the application of the systematic development of very precise instructions to a specific area of activity.

Once a successful method of accomplishing a task is developed there is the process of transferring this method to other persons and to the new generation. If the methods prove successful and useful, they may become ritualized.

Ritualization in human affairs is a very old teaching technique. The vast number of impressive drawings and paintings found in the caves of southern France and Spain may be remnants of prehistoric ritual learning devices. Like many things which are not immediately understandable they are generally considered religious, but these paintings were probably religious only in the broadest interpretation. Probably they served numerous functions, but most likely they were powerful devices for teaching the cultural nomemes for hunting the great game animals of the period. The deep dark limestone caves were school rooms, isolated, quiet, mysterious, safe from distractions, awe inspiring. Deep in these recesses the young men were malleable. There the great animals were displayed. The students learned their anatomy by study and by drawing and sculpting. They listened to discussions of their characteristics and habits. They learned the nomemes of hunting, how to approach game animals, how to detect danger signs, and where to aim their weapons. It is unlikely they had many opportunities to practice on living specimens since these were often large and dangerous mammoths, wooly rhinoceros, and great cave bears. But in the safety of the caves they could prepare themselves, they could learn, and they could share. Even today the dances of native peoples usually represent real events: hunting or corn planting or other activities vital to the group. Much of it is symbolized and foreshortened and often unrecognized, but the real life lessons are there. The concentration, the attention to detail, the forming of clear images, memorization, and testing are all woven into the rituals.

Learning, however, does not always run a simple clear course. Nonconformity and deviancy arise in every society. The relative incidence varies greatly in different societies. It is often minimal in non-industrial groups and maximal in urban commercial societies. The relationship of deviancy to the learning process raises a host of problems. Is the occurrence of learning deviancy a product of defects within the individual or of problems within the sociocultural setting? Not all individuals are born genetically and biologically exactly the same. Differences in the number, kind and location of chromosomes can be an important factor that effects the mental capacity of the individual.

Malfunctioning of the metabolic system is another. Accidents, injuries, illnesses, dietary deficiency all have their effects upon particular persons. These must be recognized for what they are. Many go undiagnosed because people have preconceptions about the causes of overt behavior. There is still a strong tendency to ascribe all behavior deviations to some kind of psychic disorder, or to racial origins. There is no evidence for any distinctive racial behavior and all normally functioning humans of whatever race appear to have roughly the same learning potential at the time of birth. The events that take place from the first minutes of life, each hour, day, week, month, year, and decade are the critical factors.

Deviant behavior is a reality. It is difficult to understand and accept. It presents a threat and a danger to the society. The deviant cannot be relied upon. He lies outside or partially outside the group. He may not have learned or is unable to learn the nomemes of behavior valued by his society. He may have learned a conflicting set of directives, or received incorrect information.

Learning a contrary or conflicting set of instructions often occurs within minority and immigrant groups and consequently transculturating individuals may suffer great conflicts. They are confused and frustrated by having to make choices between two different sets of nomemes. Their parents and relatives have given them one set, the major society and the school demand another. Sometimes they are not even aware there is a conflict and, in extreme cases, run afoul of the law. In their confusion, dismay, and frustration they feel outraged. After all they learned the cultural nomemes of behavior, of speech, of mannerism, in good faith, with the innocence and sincerity of childhood. Suddenly they are told that everything they have learned is wrong, or incorrect, and that they are ignorant or unworthy persons. They may reject both cultures and resort to basic biogenic reactions or try to develop their own set of behavioral nomemes. In any case they present a problem for the society which the society tries to solve by putting the responsibility for their deviancy back upon the individual.

This process of blaming the individual results from a failure to recognize that the most important aspect of learning is the cultural setting, the enculturation structure. In order to learn, it is necessary to have the proper conditions to learn how to learn. In modern America, where formal learning is emphasized, it is too often assumed that everyone knows how to learn by the time he gets to school. Unfortunately, this is not the case. Many children have been brought up in informal settings, where language and behavior are used primarily to convey emotional states rather than constructive information. The growth sequences in their mental maturation did not include the links and the practice whereby learning skills vital to formal education became part of their cognitive equipment. They have other kinds of skills, but these are not valued as highly or are unrelated to the formal school setting.

Enculturation consists of many processes. Observation, retention, and recall are all trained acts. The child must have nomemes for learning how to focus his attention, arousing his awareness, for developing sensory acuity. Most functioning cultural systems have established nomemes and procedures for developing these characteristics in the young generation. How well they absorb these first nomemes determines in large ,part how well they will learn more complex nomemes as they mature. Established cultures seldom have great discontinuity between stages in the child's growth, between what he has learned at one stage and what he will use at a later. His learning, while apparently simple, flows relatively smoothly through the life cycle stages in correspondence with what he already has learned and what is demanded of him. Since most of what he needs to know is being enacted all around him by people in different stages of the life cycle, imitation is an important method of his learning.

Many people cannot understand how individuals become so bound to their own culture, so emotionally rigid that they are unable to eat the food of other people or to tolerate their mannerisms and appearance. Why do people slavishly follow the existing cultural nomemes and become emotionally disturbed if they are violated or challenged? Most human beings are born within a single particular culture and they learn only the nomemes of their own group. They literally know no other manner of behaving. Often they cannot even conceive of other ways. They have been taught that their behavior is "right and proper." They have been trained to use certain cultural nomemes and these plans have been translated into habits. Obviously, they have been useful for they are demonstrated in all the living people around them. They seldom make any intellectual effort to question these nomemes; they work and they do not need explaining. They may not be able to articulate the behavioral nomemes they are using any more than most speakers can state the grammatical principles of their speech although they can use them successfully.

On the other hand, violations of the cultural plans are quite visible and often lead to disastrous results. In the Hopi desert farming community, it is critical to plant corn at precisely the right time of the year. The tragic consequences of deviation can be quickly and dramatically shown. A year without corn produces a firm belief in the principles of Hopi farming, provided the group survives.

Other aspects of Hopi culture also demonstrate the amazing persistence of culture and the power of enculturation. Generation after generation the Hopi cultural plan has been passed down relatively uncontested and unchanged. The young Hopi seldom appear to offer any resistance to the learning of these traditions. They contrast markedly with children in modern American society where it is, it seems, so often the reverse. The Hopi child is eager and proud to learn his culture and participate fully in Hopi life. He is not fearful and dismayed by the prospects for the future. He is not disappointed in his past. He feels reasonably confident and sure of his life pattern because he sees it being lived all around him. As a young boy he observes the behavior of the older children and knows that will be his behavior when he reaches their age. He sees the young man, the adult, and the old man, all with their tasks, their place, and their rewards. His worries about old age are few because the purpose of life, the nomemes that apply, and the satisfactions that are given are appropriate for each age. He looks forward to reaching each succeeding level with its new problems and its new responsibilities. For each generation, Hopi culture is replicated. Few changes are permitted and few are wanted. Rituals and situations are structured to teach the cultural plans unchanged from generation to generation. Without alternatives the young were unaware of other possibilities of behavior. All this has changed, of course, with the arrival of the American school and the middle class teacher. Hopi culture struggles to survive, the old clinging to their ways, the young sharing in their way a version of American life.

Every human being is capable of learning any culture when he is born, but once a person has learned a particular set of cultural nomemes, these tend to inhibit the use of alternate or conflicting nomemes. The initial nomemes become engraved and are almost impossible to eradicate. However, difficulties in using basic cultural nomemes usually do not arise until an individual is exposed to different patterns of behavior. At that time a person may be forced to make decisions about which nomemes to apply. He may become confused and frustrated or even unable to function.

This results because a person cannot act or do what is expected until he knows what is expected. People do not know automatically how to behave. The ability to know what is required or expected and when it has been achieved, is critical to human behavior. Without this ability successful behavior is accidental. The development of the capacity to behave according to the cultural nomemes is shaped by the ability to perceive the consequences. The effect of the consequences upon immediate behavior is related to how far apart in time the consequences and behavior are and the intensity of each.

If a person is burned each time he takes a spoonful of hot soup, he learns to wait until it cools. But he can acquire the concept of waiting in several ways. He can learn by trial, error and accident. He can observe other people waiting for the food to cool and imitate their example, or he may be directed by someone else not to eat the soup for a few minutes. In both the latter examples it is obvious that learning can take place without experiencing directly the physiological effect of being burned by the hot soup.

Immense difficulties arise in the learning process if the consequences are so far removed from the behavior that no relationship can be seen. It is difficult for a child, for example, to relate failure to brush his teeth to caries which do not appear until years later. Furthermore, this is a singular type of behavior in that by the time one understands the importance of brushing one's teeth, it is too late to do anything about it.

While understanding first time learning is diffucult enough, there is an even greater problem in understanding relearning or changing established behavior. Since whatever one learned is learned within a time frame, it is probable that much of what one learns at any particular time will have to be modified and changed as one grows older and increases his experience. This change in behavior is dependent upon either the substitution of a new cultural nomeme or the modification of the old nomeme. To change behavior then means much more than merely offering a new set of rewards. It means the cognitive restructuring of the nomemes and models that have been used to guide behavior. It is therefore important not only to understand the reward associated with the behavior, but the structure of the nomeme itself. If one drinks alcohol to excess it is not enough simply to point out the negative consequences of such behavior; the nomemes that the person is using must be altered or eliminated and this may be beyond the control of the person. A negative reward, that is immediate illness after drinking, may be used to change this behavior, for this may bring about a restructuring of the nomolary involved in drinking. While a negative value may be attached to the old behavior, success will depend upon the ability to develop an alternate or dominating nomeme that leads to more desirable behavior. One cannot simply abandon the old nomeme letting it lie in apparent disuse. The old pattern itself must be superseded by the new nomeme which is now applied in the old situation.

While all experience contributes to learning in some fashion, the life course is not determined solely by the sufferings and anguish of childhood, to the secret love of one's mother, hatred of one's father, mechanisms that writhe and retch in psychic agony. True, patterns are being etched, experiences are being coupled like the cars of an express train, baggage here, engine there. And if they are not in the proper order, if later they must be shifted and banged and jolted into new configurations, dislocation, confusion, and malfunction will surely follow. If the impact of the experience is intense, negative, or lengthy enough to start its own chain of events, then later life will undoubtedly be affected.

A child has a greater potential than adults for setting in motion damaging chains of psychic processes simply because of the lack of prior blocking experiences. This does not mean however that adult behavior is entirely at the mercy of a tyrannical event of infanthood. All experiences leave some mark on the individual, whatever the age when they occur. Consequently all have the potential of affecting all subsequent behavior. Because the individual seldom, if ever, has total control over what he is to experience, he often has no way of knowing whether a particular experience is good or bad in terms of some later evaluation.

Internal psychic mechanisms work within this frame to protect the individual and they may work independently of conscious awareness. To think, however, that the infant is jealous of his father's sexual activity with his mother is ludicrous and requires that the child have a preunderstanding of the meaning of sexual behavior, that he have a knowledge of his parents' sexual activity, and that he have some innate concept of jealousy. None of this appears to be true. While the child might be aware that his mother was devoting more of her attention than he might desire to the father, to assume that there is some psychic mechanism thereby set in motion that is somehow damaging in and of itself is without foundation.

The primary purpose of cultural learning is to enable each person to use the nomemes and plans that have already been developed and await him. These plans presuppose the existence of a social group capable of developing and maintaining these nomemes. A concomitant task then is the preservation of the social group through which the plans become meaningful. The relationship is similar to that of a man and a machine. The machine manufactures something the man needs if the instructions are followed. But another set of nomemes must be used to keep the machine itself operative. The success of all depends upon learning.

CHAPTER ELEVEN

THE CONSTANT BECOMING

Everyone must face the inevitable task of growing older. Far more is involved than merely aging however. The real problem is adjusting to the constant change in the behavioral nomemes one has spent so much time and effort acquiring. Not only must every person adjust to his own biological aging, changes in body shape, of energy levels, of interest, but he must accept the fact that he lags further and further behind the main thrust of activity occurring in his society. Buildings that he loved disappear, old friends move or die, the country-side becomes covered with houses and factories. He cannot find his way about as easily. The store where he always shopped is gone.

If one of the tasks of culture is to give stability and regularity to human life, to have the culture of one's youth disappear and be replaced by new sets of unfamiliar traits and nomemes can be a frightening and disheartening experience. Even when one's youth was not particularly happy or pleasant, the things that one learned then are the familiar ways. Older people learned the cultural nomemes of their day and time with the reasonable expectation that they were useful and valuable. Now they see them shattered and displaced by an entirely new set, by different values and moral standards, by new art forms or styles. Today's aged person has been brought up in one cultural tradition and will die in another, in a setting different in every way from what he learned to value as a child.

While this process has always occurred in every time and in every society, the rate of change has greatly accelerated in recent times. The biological generation has remained at twenty to twenty-five years but the cultural generation has grown shorter and shorter. Today in modern America, it has been reduced to a period hardly longer than five years. Young people of twenty-five are already out of touch with the eighteen-year-olds who have quickly replaced them, creating their own cultural heroes and themes. These phalanxes of generational cohorts sweep up to a crescendo by the age of twenty or so and then gradually disperse. Suddenly the young adults find it necessary to learn or relearn the conservative elements of society, how to make a living, get married, and have children. Eventually, they may rediscover what the human plan is all about as they become full adult members of society.

Every society and every set of cultural plans is in flux, changing, adjusting, growing, disappearing. Some increase in scope, in total size, some just change their shape. Every society, every culture contains the elements of divergence and convergence, conservation and change, traditionalism and progressiveness, liberalism and radicalism. The process of convergence produces nomemes that tend to conserve and strengthen those core principles of the culture. They have been the bastions of the society, those elements that made the society what it is. They struggle to maintain the status quo, the traditional forms and meanings. But like a glacier of crumbling ice, time moves on, soil becomes exhausted, resources depleted, populations grow, and new challenges must be met. The old nomemes are not doing the job. The process of divergence, of exploration, of creating new nomemes operates continually, constantly exploring the cultural potentials presented by the alterations in the environment, in the population. Tugging and pulling, convergence and divergence strain the cultural fabric which swirls along in a tension state of semi-balance between them. Despite every effort to freeze and make permanent any given moment, any tradition or value, it is apparent that no culture is stationary. Some may appear not to change, to have remained seemingly stable and unchanged for long periods of time, but their homeostatis is relative for the conservative elements always yield to change in the end.

Both processes are necessary and inevitable. The cultural plans represent the accumulated experience of the society and all that it has borrowed from others. These are the necessary requisites of life. They cannot be disregarded or abandoned too frivolously. They represent the most valuable possession, the greatest gift, the life source of the society. Without these plans the society would dissolve and disappear as an entity. The members of society must cling to their culture as firmly as shipwrecked mariners clutch their life rafts in a violent sea.

But at the same time it is necessary that adjustment be made even when such changes affect core concepts in the culture. These changes cannot be avoided. The culture must remain open and flexible enough to move toward an adjustment to continually emerging problems. To fail to change brings extinction as a society. Change is the way society renews itself.

The more integrated the nomemes of a society are, the more resistive the society is to change. It has developed the responses that solved its problems, has worked out satisfactory procedures, reached agreements. Change is not seen as necessary or valuable. Change, when it does occur, therefore, can have a very disruptive effect upon the tight knit society. A loose society, less integrated, is often more flexible, willing and able to tolerate change. The very looseness of a society indicates that either integration has not progressed far historically, that the society is disintegrating, or that so many contraditions and problems exist among its nomemes that integration is prevented. But societies themselves are not monolithic and uniform throughout. Within the society exist groups and institutions with many different degrees of integration. Integration is always relative and is never total.

While important changes occur in the demography and the environmental setting, change in the culture means change in the nomemes used by the members of the society. Cultural change has occurred when the set of nomemes individuals share in common is altered. Since no two persons ever hold exactly the same concept of any cultural plan or are able precisely to express in action any nomeme there is a constant element of alteration taking place. These variations, however, usually go unnoticed until they accumulate to a point where it is apparent that the nomeme has become significantly different from what it was at some point in the past.

Change can occur in terms of scope as the number of times a nomeme is used increases or decreases. This might take place because of increasing or decreasing population size, or because people no longer find the nomeme useful. The culture of a contemporary generation is never an exact replica of the culture of a previous generation despite the slowness of change, or how homogeneous the society. If the practitioners of a particular nomeme all pass away, a change has occurred although no living person may have altered his behavior. Some nomemes always die with the death of an aged person and this alone produces cultural drift and cultural loss.

Individuals change in other ways. They may move or migrate to other societies or into other subcultures. Persons from other cultural backgrounds may become neighbors or schoolmates, bringing new ways, and new nomemes. Individuals replace, alter, or add to their own nomemes as their personal experience changes. If the new plans are contrary or conflicting they may produce confusion and frustration in behavior.

An entire social group or tribe may move or migrate to another region or a tribe may be overwhelmed and engulfed by a larger, more powerful group. In the latter case, the conquerors usually impose their nomemes upon the dominated group which over a period of time adopts them and changes its behavior. Usually some exchange of behavioral patterns occurs both ways.

Change does not occur equally in all areas of culture. The easiest nomemes to change often are those dealing with material things, with tools, houses, roads, and bridges. Technological changes, unless they present an obvious threat, usually are additive although they may encounter resistance if they totally replace older nomemes. It generally is far more difficult to change the sociological structures, the institutions, statuses, and roles of a society than it is to change the material goods. The individual is far too committed in these areas and too emotionally involved, but if dissatisfaction is rampant and the existing social structure is failing to provide enough life satisfaction opportunities, then change will be more acceptable.

Difficult as it may be to change the sociological plans, it is even more difficult to change the behavioral nomemes in the subjective areas of life, in the values, beliefs, and religious systems. The advantages of change are never so apparent here, seldom so urgent. The emotional commitment is often intense and binding. There is less certainty about the outcome. If one abandons his gods, how is one to know what the response will be? If one's gods are as powerful as claimed, the risks are great if one forsakes them.

Language change is intimately bound to the other facts of change. It is a slow, often painful, and difficult process. Yet it occurs constantly. Internal change generally is slow enough that adjustment within generations is possible but externally induced change can be sudden and disruptive.

Probably the most difficult area of all to change is the personality structure of individuals within a society. The basic personality found within a society has tremendous tenacity. Despite outward change, subtle remnants of prior cultural commitments remain for lifetimes and for generations. Many personality characteristics of some American Indian groups apparently continue to persist despite several hundred years of contact with the white man.

Changes in material culture can originate either within the society or externally through contact with other groups. The internal processes include discovery, invention, modifications, and loss.

Discovery and invention means new nomemes are created, modification means people alter existing nomemes, and loss means the nomemes of manufacture or use are discarded or forgotten. Tools and material objects of course remain, at least for a time, but the manufacture and use of them disappears. If enough inventions and modifications occur, the culture as a whole grows or accretes and is enriched. If new tools replace the old or old tools are abandoned, then loss and impoverishment may occur. If an old man who knows how to shoe horses dies without leaving a successor, his nomemes die also and a cultural trait has passed away.

Changes brought about by borrowing from external sources involve the processes of contact, selection, and rejection. The results may be a replacement of existing traits, fusion, assimilation, or loss. Sociological changes affecting the structure of institutions, such as marriage, the family, education, or law also stem from either internal or external sources. Internal discovery of new and better ways of managing social relations may result in new nomemes that bring about structural changes or modifications. The result is increased or decreased complexity in the social structure. There may be replacement, restoration, or reconstruction of existing social institutions.

External changes in society are brought about by invasion, conquest, visiting, migration, or commerce. Voluntary borrowing of new nomemes may occur or there may be enforced change. In any case, the nomemes of an external group are used either together with the existing nomemes or in their place.

While changes in the material and sociological nomemes of culture can generally be observed in some form of physical action, this is not always so in the area of ideology where the change is primarily cognitive and emotional. Ideologies do change, but the voluntary factor is critical. Forceful efforts to bring about change in philosophy or religion meet many more difficulties whether their source is internal or external.

It is apparent that change in the cultural sense involves groups and societies. Personal and individual change is necessarily related to group change but much individual change occurs which does not become cultural. That is, the individual may develop particular behavioral nomemes which are not shared with other members of his society. This might happen if the person lived in a foreign country for a time or with a subcultural group within his own country. Changes might occur simply because of personal psychological or behavioral experience. These are often thought of as maturation, disorganization, loss, abandonment, and alienation. When these occur as observable change, they might result in some form of reorganization of the individual's behavioral activities.

Acculturation results when contact with another society bring about alterations in the nomemes of a social group. Transculturation occurs when an individual alone moves from one cultural tradition to another and is exposed to different ways of behaving. In both instances there is change in the cultural nomemes being employed. In either case there can be conflict and confusion between the old and the new nomemes especially if the new are contrary to the old. Personal and social confusion, disruption, and disorganization are often the companion of acculturation of transculturation. In acculturation, conflict may result in a split within the society between the traditional members and the progressive members. This split may simply be demographic. Cultural groups occupy spatial dimensions, and people on the margins or along major travel routes tend to have more intercultural contacts. They are exposed to more exotic behavior both sooner and in greater volume than more isolated members. They begin the process of adaptation and adjustment sooner. They are more apt to become the progressives while those with lesser contact are the traditionals. If the contact is hostile they also bear the brunt of war and attack

Conflict may occur along age lines, the older members clinging to the old nomemes, the young seeking new nomemes. This also results from the impossibility of duplicating precisely prior cultural patterns. The younger members of society, because of their youth, have not accumulated the volume of cultural knowledge and experience possessed by older members. As they age, however, their knowledge increases and is embroidered upon by their own experiences until they in turn become the keepers and teachers of cultural experience for yet a younger generation.

Cultural change is not merely inevitable, abstract, and remote. It affects directly and personally each individual. Nothing is more tragic than the estrangement that so often occurs between children and their parents because of the continuing process of change. Nothing so illustrates the results of ignorance and the failure to understand the structure of human life. Again this is not an academic argument but real behavior that produces violent acts, harsh words, destruction of the love of those one wants most to love. Children leave home in a rage, punish their parents by becoming promiscuous individuals, drug addicts, criminals, worse parents to their own children, divorced, and finally end up old and alone. Some parents punish their children, over-react to the maturation process, force them out of the home, become bitter and angry, and finally old and childless and alone. They cannot understand what has happened to destroy something that began with a genuine desire to have children, to make a decent home for them, to give them love and protection, and to see them grow up and become likeable worthwhile adults. But what so often happens is the opposite; the child grows up difficult, headstrong, rejecting the parents, ridiculing the parents' goals and values, destroying the very things the parents loved and wanted most.

The tragedy of this situation is that it is neither inevitable or universal, but results from the failure to understand the process of culture. This process includes the necessary adjustments every society must make to the world in which it exists, and the adjustments everyone must make as he passes through the various stages of the life cycle. Where these stages are clearly structured and where the environment remains relatively unchanged, people have an opportunity to understand and adjust. Children do not develop ideas and behavior that are radically different from those of their parents and they understand better why their parents behave the way they do. On the other hand, the parents do not see their children becoming more and more alienated because the children are behaving in a recognizable and desired manner.

But where the changes that are occurring in both the environmental and social dimensions of life move too rapidly or too radically for the existing cultural plans to control, where population movements bring into one arena many different cultural nomemes, all being used simultaneously, an entirely different form of social existence comes into being. When one meets everyday many kinds of people acting out of many different behavioral nomemes, one cannot become attached and committed to one form of behavior. People must remain in a state of looseness and flexibility rather than committed and certain. The rigidity and commitment of parents brought up in a monocultural tradition appears old-fashioned and foolish to the young, because in the modern society they seldom encounter a comparable situation.

In today's world we have gone beyond this because children are now being born to parents who themselves have never had a monocultural commitment and who themselves have survived by a kind of personal expediency where their individual intelligence and the accidents of experience determined the course of their lives. What the reaction of second and third generation multicultural children will produce is unknown. It is a new human experience. But perhaps the wailing and weeping over alienation and the searching for communities and communes may be an indication of the problems to come. One thing is certain--man cannot live successfully either individually or socially without a reasonably understood and accepted set of cultural plans. It is difficult enough where one does not understand the cultural plans of his society, but even more difficult if he is unaware that such things as cultural nomemes exist at all.

Each person and each generation receives an accumulated cultural heritage from the past; however, constant evaluation, selection, alteration, and synthesis occur with every act and with every individual. The process of fitting the cultural nomemes to an ever changing physical, social, and biological world is unending. Deviant responses tend to increase the number and scope of available plans. Nomemes are changed, modified, discarded, and forgotten. The continuous testing of the fitness of the cultural nomemes is balanced by the need to depend upon and reinforce them.

Culture and the generation problems can be thought of as a house. One builds a home for one's family with certain ideas about the number of rooms, their relative positions and the function of different parts. Children grow up living in the house without questioning its structure. Alterations and replacements occur as parts get tattered or worn and as family composition and needs change. Eventually the house is inherited by the children and they may rush to remodel, making the house over in the image of their own needs and perceptions, adding new wallpaper or paint, perhaps moving a wall or stair, nevertheless retaining the basic structure of the building. But as the house is passed from generation to generation each new occupant adds his layer of paint, his new wallpaper, a new alteration, until gradually the house becomes a mass of patchwork. The walls are thick with layers of fading paint, bulgy with peeling paper. Eventually the house may become so altered as to be no longer recognizable or it may even become nonfunctional and finally abandoned to the ravages of time.

The segments of a cultural system are not isolated but are interrelated through overlapping networks of behavior. They are not a mere miscellany of unrelated directives and nomemes independent and free floating. They are related to each other in effective units, patterns, and configurations. When change occurs in one area, it affects all other segments of the system. Deviations and variations can lead through the years to an unsuspected and gradual drift away from the preciseness and the meaning of the original prototypes. It is for this reason that so many societies insist upon a close reproduction of ritual, ceremonies, and material objects. They are well aware of the effect of cultural drift. Tribal members believe that the cultural goods they possess represent a satisfactory adjustment to their life situation in most instances. They fear that if variations become established there will be a loss of the necessary exactness of the cultural nomemes and a consequent disruption and disintegration of their lives. People would no longer have a basis for mutual understanding and cooperation. They attempt to freeze the nomemes by ritualization or by giving them supernatural powers, striving to hold change to a minimum. The result is only to slow the process of change, never to eliminate it.

Culture is both a system and a process. It is a system of interrelated parts and it is a process as opposed to a static condition. At any given point in time a culture is an expression of the interaction between the residual of man's past and his current situation. Because it encompasses many persons and many generations, culture transcends the individual. It may be thought of as having an existence independent of any particular person, or any individual act. Because there is a continuous process of transaction between man and his total environment and because no two men are ever in the same situation, culture is never static. It is dynamic. It is more than just the accumulated knowledge and customs man has built up through the ages. It flows through time from generation to generation, but it also extends laterally to encompass each individual in its contemporary expression. New behavior is constantly under examination, old behavior is forever being discarded on the beaches of time.

CHAPTER TWELVE
BEING HUMAN

Biology is immensely important for understanding man's existence but it is merely the preamble to human behavior, a springboard to man's humanness. Man is far more than a simple reacting organism, a living chemical. The gap between organic activity and human activity is immense. While the environment insistently presses upon him, while his biology enfolds him, man's meaningful existence is superorganic, subjective and symbolic, cognitive and memory-laden, rational and emotional.

The symbols man creates are arbitrary and meaning-less in themselves, yet they are capable of producing powerful human reactions. To say "I hate you" or "I love you" is merely to voice some sounds. Yet these sounds produce tears, violence, or sexual advances. Spoken to a Chinese or an Eskimo, they elicit no rele-vant response at all. In all ways man creates the meaning he gives to his behavior.

This meaning is conveyed through language and values. The death of a child is a relatively simple biological event. Yet to the parents it can overshadow all other things. A cow may lose a calf and a day later have forgotten its existence. It will leave no psychic scars, no nightmares, no regrets. But humans have a different capacity, a different potential. While a single

155

death may have little biological significance, the human meanings are boundless.

These human meanings are boundless because subjective states do exist for humans, and because value can be given to these subjective states. They can be identified and named and treated as if they were objective reality. The capacity to experience these states is infinite. Ambition, vengeance, distrust, truth, love, hate, aggression, are all interpretations of subjective feeling states, but their interpretation is real in its context. Humans constantly place importance on event, on emotions, on thought, on things. But this valuing is entirely internal, invisible, and unmeasurable. It may be unconscious, beneath the surface of awareness. It may be subtle and refined or obvious and blatant. It can be the quiet reaction to a sunset, a musical score, to some color splashed on canvas, or the shape of a smile. None of these have meaning in themselves. They may have no meaning for most people, but infinite meaning to a particular person.

Probably man has no choice but to give his life and his activities emotional significance. To have feelings, to be aware of them, and to deal with them is innate in humans. The individual always exists in some subjective emotional condition, and never acts out of an affective vacuum.

These expressions and interpretations of subjective states are learned. Because they are learned and private, they lend themselves to many kinds of responses and many interpretations. Because they are hidden and invisible, they are easily mistaken, distorted, exaggerated, or neglected. An individual may not understand his own feeling states, may identify them erroneously, or act them out inappropriately. Man can feel guilt, anguish, despair, uncertainty, but he does not necessarily express them everywhere in the same way. While the feeling state exists, the words that label it are merely names grappling for meaning. They are not meanings in themselves.

The meanings one gives to these aspects of life are spoken of as values. The process of giving them emotional significance is the process of valuing. Giving importance to something is the result of measuring and comparing alternative possibilities. For example, Americans value democracy over fascism, capitalism over socialism, monogamy over polygamy. One values education over ignorance and good grooming over slovenliness. More importantly, each man values his life and his own existence over others.

It is an easy step from valuing to ethical behavior, and those principles that people value are usually thought of as both good and right. Certain subjective states are thought of as having universal existence: affection, respect, well being, rectitude. They are states that everyone either possesses or strives to attain. They are the ultimate goals and guiding principles of human life.

If one examines the various cultures around the world, it soon becomes evident that different peoples attach varying degrees of importance to widely different things. While they appear to have the same general values, the specific interpretations are vastly different.

Generally social values justify the cultural behavior found in each society. Thus cultural nomemes and cultural values are interrelated. If universal values appear in different societies, it is simply because they universally increase the general capacity of the society to function. The values of enlightenment, rectitude, or wealth gives emotional support to more fundamental principles used by the society. If short hair is valued over long hair, it is not because of the short or long hair, but what these mean, the clues they provide for understanding other people. Every social system gives great emotional meaning to its basic behavioral nomemes. Because different degrees of emotion can be given to these principles, the principles can be arranged in order of their importance for those people and that society although some values seem to occur in every society.

There is a fundamental and clear distinction between values and nomemes. No value, for example, will guide you through the steps necessary to make an arrow or ride a bicycle. While both of these activities may be valued, the values themselves do not spell out exactly how one enacts these activities. No amount of value concern will enable you to ride the bicycle, but that is precisely what a set of nomemes does.

The basic principle or value of all social systems goes back to individual security or well being. This is directly related to the fundamental life urge found in all living creatures. The primary principle associated with this value is concerned with increasing life security. Nature and man have both discovered that regularity and order increases life security and decreases uncertainty, and the secondary value that universally occurs is the emphasis on regularity which itself is based on the innate capacity to recognize reoccurrences and to respond to order.

Man seeks many ways of strengthening the regularity in human affairs, including the use of values, of affection, respect, or rectitude. These values do not basically differ from other nomemes but are the products of the effort to benefit from group experience. If a person continually displays hate, rejection, and disrespect, he will likely not gain from his membership in the group. Well being, power, wealth, skill, and enlightenment on the other hand, are values that tend to increase the potential for group and individual survival.

Because of man's innate need for regularity to manage his life, he has struggled to create tools or structures that increase order. He standardizes material goods, tools, houses, roads, clothing, weapons, and food producing techniques. He has regularized the production, distribution, and consumption of goods. He has organized his groupness and his sexual and procreative life. He has developed methods for handling intra and intergroup contacts through political and legal machinery. He has developed systems of ideological and artistic expression. He has not done these things out of rectitude, altruism, and affection; rather he has discovered that those values increase the effectiveness of his other efforts to manage his life.

There is often a basic conflict between humanistic values and biological or evolutionary values. Humanistic values tend to be immediate and individually oriented. Biological values tend to be long range and species oriented. Thus the humanist is interested in preserving individual lives through medicine and other help programs. He incidentally preserves the weak and the incompetent along with the strong and able. Biology on the other hand tends to eliminate some members and thus strengthen the future of the species. Each culture sets its own limits and has approached an equilibrium with existing biological factors. When this equilibrium is interfered with too rapidly or too strongly by external events there results a change in the whole society which the society is not equipped to manage. Extensive health programs in Ceylon reduced the death rate from disease but increased it from malnutrition since no provisions had been made to develop additional food resources for the increased population resulting from the new health measures. Death from disease was acceptable and understood by the society; increased death through starvation was new and adjustments had to be made. The whole work load was also altered since infants and children were the primary beneficiaries from the new health services and the same number of working people now had to support more non-workers. This is not to imply that problems of this sort are insurmountable, although there is a limit beyond which the biological factors cannot be strained.

Because human life involves continuous contact between people, interpersonal relations are the dominant feature of most people's lives. It is for this reason that the organization of human interaction is at the core of every society's existence. This interaction takes place in an arena circumscribed by subjective feeling states, nomemes, and values.

In addition to the physical continuum of each person's life, there is the continuum of internal states expressed by value utterances. While one cannot deny the importance of the physical aspects of human life, the real problems are occurring in the verbal interchange.

These problems arise out of the inherent difficulties of conjoining subjective states, the vagueness of language, and the different degrees of importance attached to various aspects of human life.

Confusion arises when people interact in the belief they are speaking the same language when in reality they are not. The meanings of many subjective words, phrases, and gestures vary slightly but significantly enough to create ambiguity and uncertainty. The preciseness of a language may erode over time as it is softened to allow for understanding people and groups, of other languages and cultures. Meanings multiply so that each word exists in a muddy circle of variation. The logic of grammatical structure itself becomes bent and twisted, reversed and obliterated. People find themselves speaking at cross purposes, knowing something is awry, but uncertain just what it is. The meanings of subjective states and the associated values are among the first elements of language to erode, and because of their critical function in human interaction, create the greatest havoc.

One of the potential products of miscommunication is intrapsychic problems for each individual. Each person innately strives to organize his behavior and his understanding of other people's behavior into a logical system. When he cannot discern the logic in behavior or find the system, when he is constantly blocked from creating a consistent image of interpersonal behavior, he will be unable to organize the data about the world into the coherent system that he needs to guide his behavior, and his behavior will then reflect that disorganization.

This is why the treatment of subjective states is so critical and why it can become so slippery. It is man's ability to name, identify, and use in speech his inner concepts however ill perceived, however vague, that is so troublesome and so rewarding. It is names given to these states--to jealousy, infidelity, hostility, or friendliness--and the treatment of these names as reality, that allows so much possibility for misunderstanding in interpersonal relations. There is a sufficiency of real problems in the world--conflicts over limited goods, over food and wealth, fear of impending threats, anxieties over real uncertainties. But to these man adds his own misperceptions, his confusion over feeling states, the conflicts over values.

Friends in their efforts to get along, or parents in their desire to bring up their children properly create these problems. Individuals in less complex societies often are more successful than modern urban communities in managing interpersonal behavior. The social relationships have not been distorted by living among strangers, by the demands of a profit economy, and by separation from kin and family. Children are given more time and opportunity to understand the verbal and interpersonal behavior which is occurring around them. The child's pace is slow; he needs help and guidance and he needs consistency. There are far more alternative values to be evaluated, more choices to be made, in the modern society. This situation is furthered by an exaggerated concern about the sacredness of the individual in America. Individualism is encouraged because it is a basic method for the manipulation of people in the economic and political systems of modern nations.

It is critical in a commercial enterprise to increase constantly the production and sale of economic goods. A major means of doing this is to offer many alternative products and to foster the advantage of having choices, of making the buyer feel individual and special. This is a direct appeal to vanity, self-esteem, the valuing of one's self. Such competitive individualism creates an atmosphere where one purchases his self-esteem through the clothes he wears, the car he drives, or the house he lives in and thus camouflages his true worth by superficial trappings. Since the competition is endless, the commercial enterprises are the beneficiaries because such competition increases purchases and profits. Chaos and confusion are deliberately created and perpetuated to provide an advantage for the commercial operation. The automotive and clothing industries do this to perfection. In those arenas only experts can expect to know all the multitude of car models with their options and names which are changed each year so no one outside the industry can understand what he is buying.

The clothing business through its constant creation of dress fads turns millions of people into faddists who must be the first to purchase any new clothing fancy. All this is part of the manipulation of people through an appeal to their ego.

There is a vast difference between interpersonal relations in well established societies and the concept of the person in the large complex heterogenous societies of today. In the former, everyone knows everyone else and there is a far greater agreement about the behavior models being used. The kinds of interpersonal problems experienced by the members of these tribal groups are likely to be very different from those experienced in the modern society. In modern societies a large proportion of interpersonal contacts are with strangers or with people one has little knowledge about. Motives, the degree of trust, caution, all must be evaluated carefully in each situation. The mobility of people is so great that one may have no redress in event someone takes advantage of you or engages in hostile behavior, because they may be far away, or their whereabouts unknown by the time one discovers what has occurred. Therefore, one's actions and one's verbal statements are different, less direct and open than they might be in a tribal society where one knows directly the other person, his family and kin, his motives and objectives. There one has immediate recourse to retribution in the event of some type of hostile action. It is in the large heterogeneous and mobile societies that the kind of problems of interpersonal behavior so familiar in America and to the world of psychology, arise.

In simply structured societies the future behavior of each person ideally is already planned and known. The relations of the life cycle to behavior is understood. Crisis points in one's life are ritualized and shared by all. The male-female behavior patterns are structured, social status is generally clear and explicit and nomemes exist for behaving toward those lower in status, equal in status and higher in status. These are not left to chance to be resolved in interpersonal contact. This is an ideal and such a pattern of behavior is always being disrupted in varying degrees by external happenings, disasters, pressures from other groups, flooding, war or migration, but the pattern is clear. Most people have recognized the implicit danger in leaving important relations to solve themselves.

In an unstructured society where change or historic events have not permitted controlling patterns to emerge or they have been broken and disrupted, there is an entirely different story. Here we find people with many different nomemes trying to interact, with half understood nomemes and contradictions flourishing at the same time. In this situation one is uncertain of what to expect of others or how to interact with them. With uncertainty threatening, one may turn inward and become overly concerned about one's self, about others taking advantage of him, or of harming him. The language one uses may become devious, hidden, full of blockages and vagueness. One does not know what others will do with the knowledge one reveals about himself. He becomes dependent upon other clues, on clothes, appearance, outward style. One marries not because one knows anything about the other person, but because they are cute, beautiful, or handsome. The assumption is that these characteristics are signs of trustworthiness. One cannot risk telling acquaintances, friends and even relatives, intimate information, and one tends to become more and more secretive and devious. To conceal this fact and because these are thought of as undesirable attributes, one develops a public personality which smiles sincerely at you, looks you firmly in the eye, talks glibly and uses the quick handshake.

Like armor, these abilities are intended to prevent any attack however subtle from penetrating into those inner areas of one's life. So these individuals develop a behavior code which guides them in a unstable and uncertain world. They may even share this code with many others in the society. But since it is a code of expediency fashioned to guide individual and not group behavior, it is antithetical to the full rewards to be gained from the operations of a structured society. It is only a step toward the creation of a stable culture which will eventually emerge if there is some moment of historic stability. This is not to say, however, that this situation itself may not be productive both in personal life terms and in social terms.

Self-esteem becomes, therefore, a primary focus of life. It is here that humans go far beyond the other animals through their symbolizing ability and power to identify name and value. Man can label himself and distinguish himself as an individual from other humans by his name. And since he can name he can elaborate on his self-concept by adding adjectives of size, color, strength, beauty, or manliness. His name and its adjectives draw a boundary around his self and separates his body from other objects and other bodies. He can distinguish his movements from other activity and by naming, distinguish parts of his body from other parts. By using words, he draws a mental image of himself as if he were outside his body observing himself. By naming hunger, he can talk about the invisible internal state of hunger. By identifying sorrow, he can tell someone about his internal feelings. He can even talk about feelings of hunger when he is not hungry, or merely by the use of the word and what it stimulates, convince himself that he should eat. But, more importantly, he can send his self on imaginary voyages where it clashes with other selves. His self can be insulted by verbal comment. Other people talk with one's self, test it, confuse it, make overtures, reject it. To call one a coward is to do nothing but utter some words, yet these sounds because they name the self have the power to affect the self, to make one cringe or cry or be angry. Because the self is a stand-in for the life of the body, it suffers the blows that would be aimed at the flesh. But, because it is a concept, the blows are only verbal.

Nevertheless these blows are real. It is primarily through verbal exchange that people are judged. If one is thought to be neurotic or psychotic, it is usually because of the nature of the verbal activity. This is a two-pronged spear for the way one becomes psychotic may be related to the verbal experiences one has had. The old adage that, "sticks and stones may break my bones, but words will never hurt me" is erroneous. It is words that do the most damage. So, while words are only sounds, they have developed the potency to injure others as surely as darts of flint and steel. Their effectiveness is an outcome of the value man places on himself, his self-esteem. For it is this self-esteem that is the primary target and the ultimate victim of the verbal attack. It is the reality of subjective feeling states, the values that surround these states, and the attachment of these to the individual's self-concept that make verbal interaction the distinctive feature of human existence.

CHAPTER THIRTEEN

CRISIS, CULTURE AND THE FUTURE

Mankind is in crisis. The world is plagued by the realities of finite size and finite resources and by the infinite capacity for human reproduction. Competition for limited land and limited goods has created greater and greater tension within the world community. The waste produced by humans in their struggle to exist increasingly pollutes the land, the air, and the water. It is apparent to anyone that an uncontrolled continuance of the present direction of human life will shortly bring us all to the brink of disaster. This is not doomsday talk or fatalism but merely the logic of reality. The unbridled growth of human population with the resultant demand on the space, energy, food producing capacity, and natural resources of the earth will force massive changes in the level of human existence. Predicting when these changes will begin and projecting what they will be has become a favorite pastime. But the world goes on until there is some personal jolt, and suddenly there is no gasoline or fuel oil, meat or bread or electricity. Then the cries begin, but too late.

This is the story of man, as over and over again he has occupied the land and exhausted the resources, the soil, timber, wild game, fish, or minerals. In the past when human groups faced the depletion of the soil or the disaster of population growth, they picked up their baggage and moved on to begin again in greener pastures. If the pastures were already occupied, they fought and were either defeated and annihilated, or conquered and took the land. But today there are few places one can move to because man everywhere faces the same problems. The earth has at last become global; hence the problems of mankind are global. It has become increasingly difficult to push the ultimate problem on ahead into the next time period and on to the next generation. As each society is squeezed into closer and closer contact with its neighbors, the cultural systems that man has developed, the separate games that each society plays, become themselves more and more a source of conflict. It is not enough that there are the physical problems of space and resources, but to these man adds still another, problems created by his own behavior and his failure to understand that behavior.

People have little tolerance for other cultural systems; they view them with fear and suspicion. They do not understand them and feel uneasy and hostile. They confuse the people they see with the culture they enact. Since these societies are different and dangerous, it is easy to pass judgement on them and think of them as less moral than one's own, less worthy, perhaps primitive, communistic, warlike, or even subhuman. They load their conversation with words like "cannibal," "headhunter," "fascist," "Nazi," "savages," "authoritarian," "dictatorships," "socialistic." They develop exaggerated concepts of patriotism, superiority, and nationalism in response. They spend more and more of their dwindling resources on military materials and threat displays, on subversion and espionage. Twentieth century man seems determined to go down with a bang, not with a whimper after all.

As the world has shrunk smaller and smaller, as the fuse gets shorter and shorter and cultural contact more and more abrasive, the need to understand culture and cultural differences becomes more and more urgent. But because of the vast historic events of migration, war and conquest, culture as a guiding system for behaving has become less visible and less understood. People no longer are born into distinctive cultural traditions where they remain all their lives, relatively isolated from other systems. Consequently, they have an unclear grasp of the cultural plan they are using or even that such a thing as a cultural plan exists. All they see is the urbanized world with its vast mixtures of peoples, behaviors, customs, and traditions, few of which seem very appropriate for modern conditions.

Today almost everyone throughout the world is exposed to many other cultural traditions. Recently an explorer deep in the heart of the Brazilian jungles was asked by an Indian who had never traveled out of his own territory and who lived as tribally as any of his forefathers, which team had won the baseball World Series. People no longer can recognize the boundaries of distinct culture systems. They have only vague ideas of the differences between English or German or Russian or Mexican American or Black American cultures and what these mean for behavior. If they think about it at all they see the differences as national or racial and evidenced in languages or perhaps food and costumes. Because the globalization of these nations through hotel chains, travel, and films has painted a coat of superficial modernization over the underlying cultural foundations, people are no longer aware of what culture is or how it functions. Because they cannot see the cultural plans by which people are operating, they come to believe that people only act out of some private, unique, and personal mechanism. They think it is a Hitler, or a Mussolini or a Stalin who create the problems of the world and that they begin wars out of their personal ambitions or warped personalities. They extend these personality traits to the entire nation so that all Germans are compulsive or English heroic or French intellectual.

The crises are not confined to conflict between different societies, but more and more arise within societies themselves. Social class struggles, subcultural conflicts, generational quarrels, family ruptures, and individual disorders all increasingly threaten the fabric of human life. The human world is in the throes of a vast reorganization, a transformation so immense that its dimensions and its product cannot be foreseen. The symptoms are everywhere but there are few clues to the ultimate solution. The political structure of the world shifts as natural resources increase or decrease in value on the world market. With these shifts come disillusionment, loss of cultural loyalty, internal strife, rebellion, and more and more concern with personal and individual survival.

Probably every generation of mankind has faced similar problems. For example, we have ample record of Sumerian school children of five thousand years ago complaining about their lessons and teachers. Unions, pickets, and strikes were found in ancient Egypt and youth rebellions were bemoaned in classical Greece. Riots in the schools were common in Europe during the Middle Ages. Even peaceful people like the Hopi have had their quarrels and settlements. Every generation feels its own problems are the most important and pressing that ever afflicted mankind. The short span of each man's existence creates a certain urgency and egocentrism about the problems one faces. Who can today imagine the nature of personal and family existence in the Dark Ages of Europe following the breakdown of the Roman Empire? With law and order gone, bands of marauders roamed the land, robbing, looting, and raping without resistance. No city, village, or farm was safe. There was no one to appeal to, no one to ask for help. Children were seized never to be heard from again. Disease ran rampant because sewer systems were not maintained, because refugees crowded into towns and cities for safety, because crops were destroyed or stolen or never planted at all. People wandered over the face of Europe without national, tribal, or familial ties. The cultural plan had been broken, and innumerable tribal and local plans were mixed and confused into a chaos that has not been resolved to this day. Christianity arose in this vacuum and formed the nucleus for recovering a semblance of order in human existence. However, Christianity would not have been enough by itself. The saving feature of Europe was the discovery, exploration, and exploitation of the New World, Africa, and Australia. Not only did these regions pour billions of dollars worth of new resources into the economies of Europe, but they absorbed the vast overflow of population that developed during the fifteenth through the nineteenth centuries.

But today's problems can no longer be solved merely by shifting populations about, or by looting resource rich countries. They cannot be solved by waiting for nature to take its course, or by relying upon the fact that man has always solved his problems, or had them solved for him. It is no doubt true that our problems will disappear in some fashion, just as the dinosaurs' problems were resolved. However, we hope for more than this--more than mere survival, but for the creation of a full opportunity for most humans to have some human existence as well.

If the world is in crisis what is to be done? Or should anything be done? Is it possible that the way things are is the way things should be? Maybe it is not feasible or desirable to strive to improve upon the current existence of man. Many people do not believe it is either possible or desirable. They believe that this is the way the world is, that one should not fight it but learn to accept it. They regard as youthful idealism and sheer utopianism the agitation toward life improvement. In many parts of the world the national political and industrial leaders not only do not concern themselves with the plight of their fellow man but are appalled that anyone would. It does not bother them that starvation is rampant, that beggars clutter the streets, that children die of diseases and malnutrition by the thousands. That is part of life and it is beyond the control of man. It is clear that the greatest barrier to resolving the world crisis is people themselves, their ignorance, self interest, and lack of faith that man can improve his existence.

But within many men there is a constant ache, a deep concern, and a strong belief that human life can be made better. In fact the whole cultural concept rests on the premise that men do strive to improve their control over destiny, and that they can solve many of their life problems. Despite all the discoveries, inventions, and achievements of mankind, the belief persists that man has not yet reached his potential, a potential, of course, that constantly changes.

Many of the great attainments of man in recent times, have been in the physical and biological spheres, with machines, technology and medicine. There has been significantly less success in the social arena. Many social achievements in fact were made long ago. The family, marriage, political leadership and legal order are all ancient institutions. Managing society and projecting into it increased amounts of happiness and well being, themselves ethnocentric concepts, has seemed to present insurmountable obstacles. Many people may well argue that in fact the quality of life is not currently as high as it has been in certain historic periods and certain places in the world. It is this belief, this conclusion that modern man may have slipped backwards socially that lends to much of the widespread cynicism and despair.

Despite the desire for simple solutions the resolution of human problems is seldom simple. To ask for immediate and dramatic changes in behavior, for immediate solutions to international disputes, to the complex economic problems that beset the world, is unrealistic. The maladies of modern society have not just suddenly appeared like the Asian Flu or a tidal wave. These problems have been building for generations, hiding in the wings ready to emerge. What took ages to bring about, may take time to resolve. Many of these problems are generational and therefore cannot really be solved until the members of a generation pass away. Others are so complex it requires a generation to educate and train the individual members of society how to function under new cultural plans.

While all societies and all people must have some kind of nomemic plan in order to function, there is a vast difference in the efficiency and unification of different social groups. Cultural plans require reasonable adherence and commitment from the members of the society, but there is a limit to the number of individuals who can cooperate and function with any given set of cultural plans in a particular ecological setting. The larger the group the greater the inevitability of deviancy and the greater the chances for misunderstanding and malfunction. This does not mean that small groups necessarily function better than large groups, or that small groups are the human ideal. That naturally depends upon the nature of the task, the means of communication, and the amount of success and failure that can be shared. If there is only a small amount of arable land available and a relatively large population seeking to share it, then it is obvious that conflict is probable. If there is limitless land then the potential for conflict is reduced. If the problem is protection from a large powerful nation, the society must be able to muster a large defensive force or face an inevitable defeat.

Problems can be reduced in other ways if the unity and adherence to the cultural plan are understood. Many examples are known of an entire society's membership suffering great misfortunes together, or even total destruction. Belief in and adherence to the cultural plans so long as these are reasonably consonant with the existing situation is the key. While this alone may not always pull the society through a major crisis, the members themselves do not feel disillusioned with their culture. They may die fighting as the Jews did at Masada, the Sioux at Wounded Knee, but their culture was not blamed.

To comprehend the cultural crisis that faces us is to understand that culture is a system, a complex of many interrelated parts all dependent upon each other. Not only is culture a system striving to operate within the immediate world, but it functions the way it does because it is composed of the fragments of the past. It is like an old automobile that was first driven in 1920, repaired in 1925, rebuilt in 1930, overhauled again in 1950 and that now chugs along on 1970 gasoline,

1960 tires and a 1940 transmission. There can be no separation of the past from the present anymore than a man of seventy who must eat and sleep in the present can discard his years.

The most favorable human existence for most people might be found within small or medium size agricultural and largely self-sufficient villages. In these villages, with neighboring similar villages on each side, satisfactory ratios of land resources and populations could be maintained indefinitely. This group would be large enough for a variety of human relationships but small enough that most contacts could be on a familiar personal level. Everyone would be guaranteed living space and land, and the sale, accumulation, and subdivision of land closely regulated. Changing residence from village to village would also have to be regulated and balanced. Growth and change would be slow enough that it overlapped generations and people could make new adjustments without total destruction of their lives.

This style of life would not be satisfactory to all people or to all ecological situations. Nevertheless it would provide a basic level of life for a majority of people to live a reasonably happy and useful existence.

Some people would require other modes of life. The most obvious of these would be an urban environment. Regardless of how many problems large cities present, urban areas are necessary and useful. It is the dominance of urbanism over other life styles and the distortion of personal existence that must be guarded against. This requires controlling the size of cities and the proportion of the total population that can live in urban settings at any given moment. The problem with cities is the personal anonymity that often develops and the tendency of the city to become a human wastebasket where surplus rural migrants congregate, where the unemployed, the leisured, the criminal, and the incompetent gather. The size and structure of modern urban areas produces an entirely different form of human life where the factors of personal knowledge, public opinion, and kinship are no longer very effective in controlling behavior. Cities are simply too large to be self-regulating in the same way that villages are.

How then do you construct and maintain cities where the quality of life is satisfactory for all citizens? The solution that modern cities have been forced to adopt is a greater and greater degree of external control and regulation. These are expressed through increasing numbers of complex laws and regulations overseen by larger and larger numbers of police and other enforcement agencies. This direction is not only non-productive but eventuates in two camps of citizenry, one constantly watching the other, one constantly aware of being watched and manipulated. The biggest business in many cities soon becomes simply trying to maintain some semblance of social order. Most people reject this way of living, but it is a way that seems to inevitably emerge from the nature of urban life.

In attempting to develop a strategy for handling our cultural crisis one must distinguish between the construction of a social structure and the repair of such an entity. Culture is primarily a tool of construction rather than reconstruction. In those societies where the culture is understood and valued, a strong effort is constantly being made to avoid actions that will require repairs later. The effort is expended on performing correctly in the first place.

Again we may use the analogy of a building in which culture can be thought of as a growing skyscraper. Buildings can be constructed that begin without plans or foundations. Stories can be added one by one as the need arises or whims seize one. While a structure may emerge eventually, it usually is so haphazard, and ill conceived that it is dangerous to use. On the other hand, a good solid foundation can be laid out and each additional floor carefully built to stand the weight of the next, so that a very substantial building will result. Even if no one knows how many stories will be added in the future, if each floor is made in congruency with the floors above and below, and with an awareness of the strengths and weaknesses of the material employed, then the chances of a successful building are greatly enhanced.

In the development of cultural systems the nomemes and plans one begins with result not only in a certain kind of immediate human existence but provide the foundations upon which succeeding generations build their lives. The cultural plans extend through time and provide the overlap and connections between generations. Culture as a human tool depends for its effectiveness upon the fact that each behavioral act is a joint between existing cultural nomemes and the demands of the situation. These joints are the links that provide the transition from day to day, month to month, and year to year. They prevent new acts from being sudden, jarring or destructive of existing cultural plans, and consequently of people who depend upon these plans. There must be enough time, however, for externally introduced ideas to be absorbed into the basic patterns of behavior.

If we return to the game analogy, it is easy to see that each kind of game is a separate entity, a distinct unit of behavior. Football is not baseball or basketball or golf. One cannot exchange rules or equipment or activity between these games. Players who attempt to play football with different rules soon find they cannot play. If the old rules are changed, there must be enough time for the new rules to be understood and adjustments made. When rules are consciously changed, the changes are usually minor and derivative and do not alter the game significantly. The basic structure of the game remains relatively untouched.

A crisis will develop, however, if new players or referees with different ideas about how the game should be played are brought in. Players will be confused, angry, frustrated and may even refuse to play at all. Once the team begins to disintegrate, once the cohesion engendered by the commonly held set of rules is broken, it is very difficult to repair the damage.

Although cultures are much more complex than games many of the same principles apply. The limited scope of games allowed them to be analyzed, players' actions studied, errors pointed out and adjustments and repairs made. It is almost impossible, however, in a complex society to identify the causes of some behavior as distinct from the results. Criminals may be jailed, but that seldom solves the problem of why there was a crime in the first place. It is also extremely difficult if not impossible to repair a cultural system that has begun to totter and fall apart. That is the situation of most societies today.

The first task and perhaps the most important is to reestablish the fundamental understanding of the nature and function of culture. If we do not have an adequate theory of human behavior then it is impossible to take the next step. This does not mean a fanatical revival of patriotism or nationalism or a belief in any particular cultural system. The crucial point is to understand that all men and all societies are dependent for their human existence upon a shared set of cultural plans. For each individual these nomemes are the most important thing he owns for they are the passport enabling him to relate to others.

Each person who shares in these cultural plans must understand that culture is only an effective tool so long as there is agreement about its nomemes and so long as there is commitment to their meaning.

Although cultural systems exist which do not appear to be effective and which do not appear to benefit a large share of their adherents, these systems are in themselves neither good nor bad. Some societies seem to be more successful than others. Some systems can be seized by power groups and manipulated for private purposes that don't benefit the mass of citizens. Likewise cultural systems may become old and ill and malfunction. Culture is a tool and like any tool it can be misused. But in general most cultural systems tend to eliminate the malfunctions and move toward a structure of reasonable efficiency and stability within the limits of the environmental situation.

Agreement about the cultural plans and commitment to them are vital to any society and cannot be edicted. Once agreement is broken or commitment weakened, social difficulties multiply. The task in modern America is to learn how to function as a nation where there is widespread disagreement about what constitutes proper behavior, and a lack of commitment to traditional cultural plans. But what is even more threatening is a lack of awareness of the importance of understanding culture, or where there is some inkling of understanding, a belief that culture is the culprit behind the crisis. This is the crux of the problem in most modern societies.

Failure to have a common understanding comes about because people are brought together from many distinct backgrounds, with different religions, national, and racial origins. It comes about because people do not learn the basic cultural plans or these plans and their implications are not understood. It comes about in large modern nations because of the sheer impossibility of getting any large number of people to agree on anything. Nor is it clear how much disagreement is useful, healthy, or can be tolerated in a society.

Commitment refers to the degree of emotional attachment an individual has to his cultural nomemes. Commitment results from deep encultration, long practice, and fulfillment of its promises. Commitment to one's own culture comes automatically when it is the only culture one knows. One perceives oneself as a full-fledged participant without which the society could not function, and equally where the individual could not survive without the society. But such commitment has the limitation of parochialism, ethnocentrism, and prejudice.

On the other hand, too great an exposure to other social systems without understanding the structure of culture, creates the danger of presenting too many alternatives and raising doubts about the validity of one's own society. Cultural boundedness and ethnocentrism cannot be discarded as simply useless and damaging behavior; they have their place.

Nevertheless, it is possible to create a global culture, an awareness of cultural variation, of the necessary function of culture which can free one from the restrictions of one's limited culture without destroying oneself. The over-exposure and acceptance of other cultures that can lead to apathy, disdain, and even hostility can be avoided in today's world with its entirely new modes of transportation and communication. In the past this kind of attitude was impossible or very limited. But it is a new world fraught with new possibilities both for destruction and creativity. The possibility for world understanding will be increased only when there is a better understanding of the nature and function of culture.